LEGAL LITERACY PROJECT

Civil Law
AND THE
Civil Justice Process

A GUIDE TO SELF-REPRESENTATION

MATTHEW MADDEN

To request permission, contact the publisher at matt@legalliteracy.com

Ebook ISBN: 979-8-218-11200-4
Paperback ISBN: 979-8-218-11201-1

Library of Congress Control Number: 2022922009

First edition: 2022

PUBLISHER:
Legal Literacy Project, LLC
Newport, Rhode Island

A Legal Literacy Project Title

https://legalliteracy.com/

To my Mom—
who taught that when you combine
unconditional love with purposeful resilience
you change lives for the better.

To my Dad—
who taught me that when you combine
unconditional love with a forgiving sense of humor
you change lives for the better.

To Karri—
who taught me to find the place where your
greatest gift meets the world's greatest need.

Table of Contents

Appendix

"Each time a man stands up for an ideal, or acts to improve the lot of others, or strikes out against injustice, he sends forth a tiny ripple of hope"

— ROBERT F. KENNEDY

Disclaimer Notice: An Explanation

"This facility does not assume any responsibility or liability for any vehicle or its contents while parked on this property."

This seemingly innocuous grouping of words—in legal parlance referred to as a *disclaimer*—can be found in parking garages, playgrounds, and public spaces all over the world. The goal of a legal disclaimer is to limit one party's liability regarding potential damages in a civil proceeding.

From an author's perspective, the legal disclaimer page is typically an afterthought of a task not often related to the primary focus of the book. In the case of this book, the legal disclaimer presents our first opportunity to gain insight into the psychology of civil litigation.

In this example, the parking garage is attempting to proactively prevent the filing of a lawsuit with regard to any stolen or damaged property that may occur in their facility. The display of a legal disclaimer clearly visible to customers is basically a proactive gambit. The message conveyed is, essentially, it's not our fault. If your car or its contents gets stolen or damaged, don't blame us and—most importantly—don't bother filing a lawsuit in an attempt to recover damages as a result of any incident that may occur on our property.

Given the intent of this book, I'd be remiss not to include my own legal disclaimer. Of course, it's not always easy to parse legal text so I'll also provide a translation.

The legal disclaimer below states that this work is intended as information, not advice. This is a critical distinction and an example of the importance of details and nuance in the practice of law. This book is not legal advice, nor should it be considered a substitution for legal advice or the need to seek legal counsel. The intention of this book is to provide the non-lawyer with a basic understanding of the emotional, psychological, and strategic factors and legal mechanics involved in pursuing civil litigation. It's designed to augment a layperson's efforts and interactions with their attorney and certainly not intended as a replacement of or substitution for your lawyer.

The translation above and the disclaimer below convey this sentiment in no uncertain terms. The complexity of civil litigation demands experience and expertise. It's not possible for any book to displace the valuable advice and judgment of an experienced attorney or team of attorneys. If you do forgo the benefit of legal counsel and attempt to wage your own arguments simply with the information contained within this book, you won't be fully capitalizing on the rights afforded to you as a citizen. Not only is this a disservice to your case, it's a threat to the civil litigation system as a whole. Truth and justice are only available to us if we correctly exercise the right and ensure the system doesn't atrophy.

In other, less lofty words, use this book as it's intended. If you fail to do so, the author will not be held responsible for such foolhardy behavior.

In the interest of transparency, this begs the question of enforceability. In the example of the parking lot, does a disclaimer exempt the parking lot owner from liability for actions that occur on his property?

As is the case with many aspects of the law, the short answer is, it depends. The issue of bailment—the transfer of property from one party to another without a transfer of ownership—is a critical factor. Other variables that may bolster or hinder either side's case include considerations such as the number of attendants on site, the attendant's ability or inability to observe the vehicles, the existence or non-existence of barriers on the parking lot, the effectiveness of such barriers, and the facility's hours of operation.

What's the primary lesson hidden in the slew of possible details? The best way to win a lawsuit is to ensure the other party never files a complaint. As an introduction to the law, this is an invaluable insight. The framing of an issue can be as important as the existence of evidence. An individual's case may rely on evidence, or more likely the various interpretations of the same evidence, but the narrative that explains this evidence is equally important. A proactively displayed legal disclaimer is, at its heart, an attempt to frame the narrative and influence the behavior of potentially adverse parties. Viewed from this perspective, the legal disclaimer may be considered by some as a misdirection intent on dismissing a case prior to the examination of any relevant facts and evidence *or* a valid, straightforward explanation of the relationship between two parties.

It depends on your perspective. The same can be said for most any issue related to the law.

Legal Disclaimer

No advice: This book contains general information about legal matters. The information contained within is not advice, and should not be treated as such.

Limitation of warranties: The legal information within this book is provided "as is" without any representations or warranties, express or implied. The author makes no representations or warranties in relation to the legal information contained within this book.

Without prejudice to the generality of the foregoing paragraph, the author does not warrant that:
- the legal information within this book will be constantly available or available at all or
- the legal information within this book is complete, true, accurate, up-to-date, or non-misleading.

Professional assistance: You must not rely on the information within this book as an alternative to legal advice from your attorney or other professional legal services provider.

If you have any specific questions about any legal matter, you should consult your attorney or other professional legal services provider.

You should never delay seeking legal advice, disregard legal advice, or commence or discontinue any legal action because of information within this book.

Liability: Nothing in this legal disclaimer will limit any of our liabilities in any way that is not permitted under applicable law, or exclude any of our liabilities that may not be excluded under applicable law.

The disclaimer language above was developed with a Contractology template and republished with a creative commons license.

A Client's Guide to Self-Representation:
The Mission

"I see, these books are probably law books, and it is an essential part of the justice dispensed here that you should be condemned not only in innocence but also in ignorance."

— FRANZ KAFKA, THE TRIAL

If you're like me, your introduction to the civil justice system was completely unexpected and a result of circumstances completely out of your control. A document— legal, official and intimidating— arrives in the mail demanding, in **bold**, a response to allegations of your alleged bad acts. Alternatively, you're the person who filed the lawsuit— the sender of the intimidating letter— when you considered all the ways you could respond to another party's bad actions and realized the legal system was the least worst of your bad options.

Whether you're the plaintiff or the defendant, if you're reading this book you're likely unfamiliar with the strategies, tactics, and mechanisms that guide and govern the civil courts in the United States. When I unexpectedly found myself faced with the choice of whether or not to investigate wrongdoing associated with my father's estate after his death, I spent countless sleepless nights seeking to educate myself about the law. In short, I understand the feelings of helplessness and hopelessness that arise when you have a suspicion that you're unprepared for an imminent legal altercation. My sleepless nights were filled with frantic Internet searches and deep dives into archaic legal concepts as I attempted to educate myself for the overwhelming experience in front of me. If you're reading this during your own bout with insomnia, please know that I can empathize with your dilemma.

By design, the civil legal system is intimidating, antiquated and—in my experience—at times purposefully confusing. The result, if not the intention, is to prevent individuals without a legal education from understanding how to navigate the maze that is the court system. The lack of familiarity with legal strategies, tactics, and concepts combined with the increasing trend of litigants representing themselves leads to confusion and uncertainty about the legal process, inefficient use of the court's time and—ultimately—poor legal outcomes.

> " By design, the civil legal system is intimidating, antiquated and—in my experience—at times purposefully confusing."

I wrote this book from the perspective of a former litigant who was once in the position of needing to educate myself about a complicated topic that I had limited interest in—until I had no choice but to become consumed by. The intended audience for this book is individuals without a legal education who find themselves in the unenviable position of needing to learn the law and understand your lawyer. This book is the information I wish I had access to, in one central resource, during my many sleepless nights as I was educating myself on the intricacies of the legal system. I trust this information will assist you as well in your pursuit of justice.

A Client's Guide to Self-Representation:
The Audience

"Unless someone you like cares a whole awful lot,
nothing is going to get better. It's not."

— DR. SEUSS (THEODOR SEUSS GEISEL), *THE LORAX*

This book exists to help people save time and money. More specifically, it's written for people representing themselves in civil court—currently or in the future—to save time and money but—given the sizable percentage of the population involved in civil litigation at one point during their lifetimes—we're all potential litigants. Most of these litigants are not attorneys, have limited to no experience in civil procedure, and have limited information regarding even the most basic tenets of civil law. This startling deficit in legal knowledge means litigants need to spend their own time or money in quickly obtaining a legal education. This is typically done via their own independent research, through discussions with attorneys, or a combination of both. As a plaintiff in an estate and trust administration and probate case, this was my legal education process. This book is intended to supplement, not replace, that process. Independent, customized research and in-depth conversations with legal experts are required when approaching any legal matter. By allowing readers to gain a basic understanding and framework of the civil legal system, the goal of this book is to inform potential litigants' approach to self-education and optimize the independent research that's a critical component of the development of a successful legal and litigation strategy. That's my definition of success for this text.

Increasing access to information saves money by decreasing the required time—via either independent research or legal fees—to understand a legal issue and, potentially, develop a litigation strategy. By increasing the layperson's understanding of the topics detailed in this book, potential litigants are effectively saving money by eliminating the effort to independently understand such issues or reducing the time spent discussing these issues with various legal experts. From the perspective of a self-represented litigant, it's surprising to discover the amount of information that can be gathered via exploratory conversations with lawyers—who may be particularly forthcoming as they view these types of discussions as the best method for finding new clients. Topics explored in this book include the following:

- The methodology for determining whether or not you have a legal cause of action or, if you're a defendant, determining if the opposition has a valid legal complaint
- The difference between a legitimate grievance and an actionable legal complaint
- The concepts of burden of proof and preponderance of the evidence that are the cornerstone of all legal matters
- The discovery process within the civil courts and the opportunities available to obtain evidence and meet the burden of proof
- The importance of legal specialties and relevant experience as it relates to your legal issues
- An explanation of each stage of the litigation process including the evaluation of a potential legal complaint, the discovery process, mediation, trial, and various resolutions available within the civil legal process
- The various interested parties involved in the litigation process and an exploration of each party's converging and oppositional motivations
- The psychological, emotional, and interpersonal factors to be weighed when considering a legal action
- Negotiation tactics to maximize your position and seek the most favorable result

- An overview of the difference between civil and criminal law and the factors to consider in a civil action as it relates to criminal issues (including criminal referral)
- A collection of additional resources that may assist your legal efforts

It's important to remember the exploration of the above topics in this book has been written from the perspective of a fellow litigant with a limited understanding of legal issues prior to my own foray in the civil justice system. I was once in your situation—facing a potential legal issue, uninformed and confused about where to seek information and advice, needing help and not knowing where to find it, and intimidated by the uncertainty of a lengthy legal battle and the related cost of waging that battle. Most importantly, this book is written from a perspective of empathy.

I know from experience that fighting a legal battle is not for the timid or faint of heart. I trust the lessons I've learned—imparted in these pages—will be of value to you as you fight your own legal battle and seek a fair and equitable resolution.

Author's Note

*"I guess the only time most people think about
injustice is when it happens to them."*

— CHARLES BUKOWSKI, *HAM ON RYE*

Some people learn the law from law school, others from necessity. I never attended law school, don't have a legal degree and never even had a particular interest in the law ...until I had no choice but to cobble together my own legal education.

After my father's death, I was involved in a lengthy and complex legal battle regarding his estate. Multiple lawyers, a wide variety of legal strategies, significant capital and a considerable commitment of my own time were required to reach a resolution. A fair monetary settlement, a more complete understanding of my father's true intentions and insight into the actions undertaken to obstruct those intentions were the defining goals of the various legal approaches I pursued. The goals were clearly understood but the ways and means of achieving the goals were a mystery.

This was my introduction to the world of civil litigation.

Litigation can be a daunting experience in the best of circumstances – though, in fairness, there's never a "good time" to be involved in a lawsuit. A sense of helplessness and isolation can infect even the most self-sufficient and assured. To the uninitiated, the lack of information extends from the legal process itself to the motivations of the various interested parties. Litigation demands the precious resources of time and money without a clear understanding of the potential return on investment for either of those commodities or even an expectation to understand the facts and learn the truth—which is ultimately the outcome most desired by litigants. The circumstances of my own experience with civil litigation, by virtue of the disputed matter, involved death and money. Given most people approach both of these topics with an abundance of caution, this only amplified the emotional toll of civil litigation.

It's safe to say the time between my father's initial diagnosis and the ultimate conclusion of the litigation related to his estate was one of the most stressful periods of my life. It was an emotional roller coaster marked by periods of hope and despair, determination and acceptance with radical changes in perspective in relatively short timeframes. After my father's death, the prospect of prolonged litigation required learning to live with an emotional burden rather than being defined by it.

I founded the Legal Literacy Project to share the lessons learned and the perspective gained in my own experience navigating the civil legal system. Any client new to the field of law is inherently operating without perfect and/or complete information despite the attempts of even the best and most communicative attorneys. The complexity of the legal system, the money required to participate in the process and the myriad of confusing and seemingly contradictory legal options available combine to place the legal novice at a significant disadvantage.

The goal of this effort is to, at least in part, provide a foundation for individuals who suddenly have an urgent need to understand the law. Written from the perspective of a client – rather than a lawyer – for current and future legal clients, this series of books are designed to be a reference for individuals propelled into the world of litigation. It's the information I wish I had when I started my legal education soon after my father's death.

The Lawsuit Stigma

"But by this time I was acutely conscious of the gap between law and justice. I knew that the letter of the law was not as important as who held the power in any real-life situation."

— HOWARD ZINN, *YOU CAN'T BE NEUTRAL ON A MOVING TRAIN: A PERSONAL HISTORY OF OUR TIMES*

"We're not the type of people to get involved in that, we're not the suing type."

The sentiment is understandable. Stories of frivolous lawsuits proliferate—both true and urban legend. Every few years, we're inundated with political commercials demonizing "greedy trial lawyers." Corrupt judges are frequent fodder for afternoon crime shows. Not to mention the general distrust of lawyers evidenced in a wide variety of public opinion surveys. Newspapers and the Internet are filled with stories that convey the compromise and inequity rife within our criminal justice system. There's a widespread, and well-founded, perception that corporations have the financial resources to fully utilize legal and litigation options while the common person lacks the money, knowledge, or network to even participate.

It's not surprising people simply don't want to get involved in a civil legal system considered, at best, dysfunctional and, at worst, fraudulent. It's not surprising so many people consider themselves "not the suing type."

Yet, this doesn't convey the whole story.

A mentality continues to pervade our culture that clear-thinking, honest people can communicate their differences in a mature manner and reach a resolution without resorting to legal means. Alternatively, others consider the legal system as the dominion of the weak as they seek to "settle their scores man-to-man." Both sentiments are misguided and equally dangerous.

The reality is not every person is truthful and/or capable of compromise and authentic communication. And not every situation will be resolved with threats and intimidation (it should go without saying that this should not be a strategy for any situation in a civil society); or even direct conversation. Disputes arise and the civil legal system was created to encourage their fair and equitable resolution.

The lawsuit stigma actively discourages participation in the civil litigation process—as much, if not more, than the perception of dysfunction. Ultimately, this stigma has a profound effect on the functioning of our civil society. This stigma effectively limits the individual's legal rights, access to legal recourse and, potentially, fairly entitled damage awards. This is done *voluntarily* for the simple reason that many individuals don't want to be burdened with the social stigma of a lawsuit. Many people just don't want to be labeled as the suing type.

> " *The lawsuit stigma actively discourages participation in the civil litigation process—as much, if not more, than the perception of dysfunction. Ultimately, this stigma has a profound effect on the functioning of our civil society."*

Of course, the decision to pursue legal action or to proactively settle a complaint is, in the best circumstances, a business decision that should be made based on a return-on-investment calculation. Yet, the stigma of pursuing recourse via legal means fundamentally alters this calculation and influences the decision-making criteria. Not only does this stigma interfere with sound business decisions, it also impacts the civil system's ultimate goal of producing just outcomes.

As flawed as the civil courts and litigation process may be, civil litigation is a hard-fought right that should not be voluntarily surrendered due to misinformed cultural pressures. Similar to muscles, rights that aren't exercised atrophy. In many cases, the folks disparaging the civil court system and discouraging its use espouse their opinions without the benefit of personal experience or may seek to perpetuate the lawsuit stigma for their own, self-serving purposes. Additionally, the corporations that influence ballot initiatives and legislation designed to minimize access and damages don't hesitate to leverage their own legal teams and take full advantage of the civil law system when it furthers their own interests. A wide variety of factors need to be considered when evaluating an individual's potential legal remedies, but the lawsuit stigma should not be one of them.

> *As flawed as the civil courts and litigation process may be, civil litigation is a hard-fought right that should not be voluntarily surrendered due to misinformed cultural pressures."*

This begs the question of who is the "suing type?" Well, we all are under the proper circumstances. As is our right.

Personal Advocacy: How to Represent Yourself in Successful Litigation

"I not only have the right to stand up for myself, but I have the responsibility. I can't ask somebody else to stand up for me if I won't stand up for myself. And once you stand up for yourself, you'd be surprised that people say 'can I be of help.'"

— MAYA ANGELOU

Due to an appalling lack of data collection—particularly at the state level—it's difficult to determine specifics regarding the number of civil lawsuits filed in federal and state courts annually in the United States as well. Experts estimated that the number of lawsuits filed annually in the country's federal and state civil courts is between fifteen and nineteen million with trends indicating an increase in filings in many jurisdictions. The National Center for State Courts in a study[1] conducted in 2015 found that approximately 25% civil defendants are representing themselves in response to a civil complaint. As recently as 1992, the National Center for State Courts had found that nearly 100% of civil defendants had chosen to engage an attorney. In an article from Bloomberg Law[2] published in 2019, a dozen experts were interviewed regarding the self-representation trend and all confirmed the increase in civil defendants representing themselves has continued since the study from the National Center for State Courts published in 2015. Unfortunately, it's clear that success in the civil courts in closely associated with hiring an attorney—and failure is more likely when a litigant is

---

[1] https://www.ncsc.org/__data/assets/pdf_file/0020/13376/civiljustice-report-2015.pdf

[2] https://news.bloomberglaw.com/us-law-week/going-to-court-without-a-lawyer-is-new-normal-for-u-s-litigants

self-represented—which has led to concerns regarding the effectiveness in the civil court's efforts to deliver justice in a system where the litigants are not equally prepared to participate.

> ❝ *Unfortunately, it's clear that success in the civil courts in closely associated with hiring an attorney—and failure is more likely when a litigant is self-represented—which has led to concerns regarding the effectiveness in the civil court's efforts to deliver justice in a system where the litigants are not equally prepared to participate.*❞

If you're considering, or have already decided, to represent yourself in civil court, you're assuming the dual responsibilities of ensuring you put forth the most compelling legal argument given the facts and circumstances of your case while also managing the emotional burden of resolving a dispute within the confines of the civil justice system. The fallacy of a client being relieved of the emotional burden of a lawsuit by their attorney has been perpetuated in a wide variety of legal thriller films. The best examples of the genre—*Philadelphia, A Civil Action,* and *Erin Brockovich*—all feature epic civil litigation crusades with extraordinary attorneys (and, in the case of Erin Brockovich, an extraordinary paralegal) who felt so compelled by the righteousness and moral underpinnings of their respective cases that their efforts became all-consuming. Yet, by opting to not hire an attorney you've decided the best advocate for making *your* argument is yourself. This is likely true whether you choose self-representation or decide to hire an attorney. It's unlikely that any lawyer you hired would dedicate his life to the pursuit of truth and justice embodied by the issues at stake in *your* case anyway. After all, not every case combines compelling legal issues, exceptional individuals, and the dramatic narrative arc needed to inspire a filmmaker.

You should hold yourself, as your own best advocate, to a high standard but there's no reason to despair if—as a self-represented litigant—your legal work doesn't inspire a blockbuster film. Your goal as a self-represented litigant is to beat the odds stacked against you—the odds stacked against all self-represented litigants—and litigate a case with a level of professionalism that makes the other participants in the case forget that you're not a lawyer.

The best lawyers demonstrate an impressive recollection of the facts, details, and legal intricacies of each case they represent and an ability to develop a winning strategy from such details. Your goal is to emulate this behavior. Your investment in civil litigation may be simply financial, but often the motives for pursuing a case extend far beyond any dollar amount. Despite the well-worn legal advice to focus on the financial return of your civil litigation investment, it's inevitable that all manner of emotions, relationships, and expectations will impact your accounting when examining your own litigation investment.

> *" The best lawyers demonstrate an impressive recollection of the facts, details, and legal intricacies of each case they represent and an ability to develop a winning strategy from such details. Your goal is to emulate this behavior."*

At a bare minimum, you need to meet the legal requirements codified within the rules of civil procedure. The production of relevant documentation and the disclosure of all the relevant facts and circumstances in an accurate manner are fair expectations of opposing counsel—and legal requirements of the court.

From a practical perspective, project management skills are essential. It's important to create and maintain your case file with copies of every piece of documentation, maintain a calendar of all relevant past and present dates, document all facts and events, and educate yourself as much as possible in every aspect of the court case including germane statutes, applicable case law, and the legal process as a whole. If you've decided that self-representation is your best course of action, the scope of your role extends far beyond project management. Ultimately, the implications of the final result—and, by extension, the responsibility—rests with you! Hiring a lawyer is essentially hiring an advocate to tell your story. You've decided to hire yourself as your own best advocate—make sure you're in a position to act as such. This book was written to assist you in this journey.

The Rise of the Self-Represented Litigant and the Financial Burden of Obtaining Representation

The Sixth Amendment of the Bill of Rights—the bedrock of criminal law in the United States— states the following:

> In all criminal prosecutions, the accused shall enjoy the right to a speedy and public trial, by an impartial jury of the state and district wherein the crime shall have been committed, which district shall have been previously ascertained by law, and to be informed of the nature and cause of the accusation; to be confronted with the witnesses against him; to have compulsory process for obtaining witnesses in his favor, and to have **the assistance of counsel for his defense.**

Yet, the guarantee to assistance of counsel does not extend—and is far from guaranteed—in the arena of civil law. Activists who focus on legal reform have raised objections to this fact given the impact the results of a civil lawsuit potentially have on individual lives. The civil justice system decides matters related to divorce, the custody of children and child support, housing issues including eviction and foreclosure, consumer protection issues and employment matters. Consumer issues associated with debt and bankruptcy, access to public benefits—such as welfare, social security, Medicaid and food stamps—injury issues related to car accidents, medical malpractice—and any of the other myriad ways humans have devised to hurt each other over the years are all decided in the country's civil courts. Some of the most complicated issues governed by civil justice proceedings include property matters, probate cases and guardianship issues. The list is as long and varied as the human imagination with the undeniable conclusion that a wide variety of important life matters are only resolved as a result of the proceedings within the confines of the civil justice system. Given the scope of civil justice matters, it's easy to understand how the result of a case heard at a civil court can, potentially, have a life-altering and permanent impact.

> *Given the scope of civil justice matters, it's easy to understand how the result of a case heard at a civil court can, potentially, have a life-altering and permanent impact."*

In 1963, the Supreme Court ruled in the case of *Gideon v Wainwright* that states are required to provide criminal defendants with a defense attorney when the defendant is charged with a serious crime and the defendant can not afford a lawyer. The phrase "you have a right to a lawyer and—if you cannot afford one—one will be provided to you" probably sounds familiar from any number of television shows or movies that include this jewel of legal arcana in their scripts. The *Gideon* decision is the basis for this right to which all citizens of the United States are entitled. Given the ubiquity of the phrase in popular culture, many people mistakenly believe this right-to -counsel applies any time a person appears in a courtroom. The right to an attorney is limited to criminal matters and only applies to matters governed by civil courts in certain circumstances with each state governed by its own laws on the matter. The National Coalition for a Civil Right to Counsel[1] offers an interactive database that enables the public to determine if a civil right-to- counsel exists based on the subject matter and jurisdiction of the case. There are certainly matters in which a party is able to invoke this right and it's worth verifying whether or not you may be eligible to demand the state provide an attorney to you free of charge. For example, a few cities and states have passed tenant right to counsel laws[2] or similar right-to-counsel laws in matters related to parental rights cases, child custody matters, abuse/neglect matters but this is far from a universal right in civil court. In the vast majority of the millions of civil lawsuits filed in federal and state courts in the United States each year, there is no right-to-counsel in civil court.

As a result, both plaintiffs and defendants either choose to self-represent or are left with no choice but self-representation in order to access the civil justice system. Not surprisingly, this choice is often based on money and—given the financial realities—it's often a reasonable decision, or at least appears to be reasonable particularly in the beginning of a lawsuit, especially for inexperienced litigants. It's not unusual for even the most inexperienced of attorneys to charge an hourly rate of $300 or more—depending on many factors such as educational background, legal experience and firm reputation—as well as demand a retainer (potentially $5,000 or more) in order to accept a case and begin legal representation. Given the complexity of the civil legal process, $300 per hour of legal work can quickly add up to thousands of dollars in legal fees. This dynamic impacts all but the most wealthy in our society. Low-income individuals and families may struggle to raise the initial $5000 retainer fee—nevermind maintain payments for legal services

---

[1] http://civilrighttocounsel.org/map

[2] http://civilrighttocounsel.org/highlighted_work/organizing_around_right_to_counsel

that can quickly add up to thousands of dollars over the course of a few short months. If you aren't able to maintain legal payments, your lawyer can petition the court for removal as your lawyer based on a lack of payment. There are certain circumstances where the lawyer is restricted from this action—and must maintain representation—but this issue, like so many matters related to the civil justice system, is complicated and attorneys have a vast advantage over their clients when evaluating the applicability of such laws to the circumstances of a particular client and case.

Middle class individuals and families—defined by the Pew Research Center as annual income of $65,000 for a family in 2021—may also struggle to pay legal fees for a complex case after even a few short months or a year of legal representation depending on the complexity and circumstances of the case. Of course, this dynamic applies to both parties in a lawsuit as depositions, hearings, motions and counter-motions accumulate developing a sunk cost mentality for the litigants while increasing the legal fees for the legal teams of both parties. The phrase "nobody wins, but the lawyers" is easy to understand given the realities of legal representation within the civil justice system.

From the perspective of a lawyer, legal firms ultimately exist to operate as profitable businesses. Lawyers understand the financial burden placed upon litigants in the civil justice system and evaluate clients based on an ability to pay their bills. Additionally, as mentioned previously, there are millions of lawsuits filed each year. The best law firms have the advantage of being selective when evaluating whether or not to represent a new client—which effectively places the burden on the client to convince a prospective lawyer to accept the client's request for representation. In other words, clients are required to prove their case—or at least convince an attorney who understands the law much better than the clients of the merits of the case—before agreeing to accept to represent the client.

It's not surprising that an increasing number of individuals have determined the best course of action when faced with a legal dispute in the civil courts is self-representation. This decision may, in the short-term, address the financial difficulties associated with obtaining effective legal counsel but surfaces its own set of challenges as self-represented litigants navigate their way through the complex maze that is this country's civil court system.

> *In other words, clients are required to prove their case—or at least convince an attorney who understands the law much better than the clients of the merits of the case—before agreeing to accept to represent the client."*

Self-Representation in Civil Court: Barriers and Challenges

The assumption inherent in the design of civil procedure is that every litigant will arrive in court with a lawyer. If you consider the arcane—and, seemingly, arbitrary—nature of civil procedure and the complexity inherent in navigating even the simplest of disputes through the array of rules, procedures and norms that comprise daily life within our civil courts, the only reasonable explanation is the presumption that every litigant has a lawyer trained in the esoteric language and customs that govern behavior in this specialized arena.

Of course, millions of litigants each year don't hire a lawyer and decide self-representation is the best course of action for their case. Experts estimate that up to 75% or more of civil cases in federal and state courts include one self-represented litigant. As previously discussed, money is a primary motivator in deciding to self-represent. In addition to the struggle to fund a civil lawsuit, many individuals—ironically—have too much individual or family income to qualify for assistance provided by legal aid organizations. In other words, many individuals and families don't have sufficient financial resources to hire an experienced attorney and have too much money to qualify for legal assistance.

> *The assumption inherent in the design of civil procedure is that every litigant will arrive in court with a lawyer."*

The choice for many individuals and families is either to self-represent or not participate in the civil justice system. As a potential plaintiff, this decision may effectively result in a person or family who does not invoke their rights due to a lack of financial resources. As a defendant, financial constraints may prevent you from raising a valid argument to a deficient—or even frivolous—legal complaint. In either situation, the result is an individual's voice being taken away and justice not being served.

Litigants who proceed in a self-represented fashion are at a distinct disadvantage. One study from the Chicago-Kent College of Law[1] found the typical litigant must perform approximately 200 distinct tasks over the course of a civil case. Procedural requirements vary from the mundane to the nerve racking. Filing a motion or pleading in the proper format, ensuring proper communication with the opposing party and the court, scheduling depositions and hearings and managing the various deadlines imposed by the civil rules of procedures all present an inexperienced litigant with countless opportunities to lose a case through a technicality, poor litigation strategy or—in some egregious examples—mistakes that would amount

---

[1] https://scholarship.kentlaw.iit.edu/cgi/viewcontent.cgi?article=1572&context=fac_schol

to legal malpractice if a licensed attorney was responsible for the same action, or lack of action.

If a self-represented litigant is able to navigate the myriad rules and procedures that govern the civil justice process, the core responsibilities of an attorney still need to be properly assumed and executed. One of the most challenging aspects of litigation is synthesizing the various pieces of evidence introduced—both favorable and unfavorable—into a digestible narrative that can be easily conveyed to the court. A primary difference between a trained lawyer and a self-represented litigant is the ability of a seasoned litigator to present a case that is easy-to-understand, inclusive of all legally relevant details and compelling. The goal is to enable the judge or jury to understand the story—from a legal perspective—and recognize a path towards deciding in your favor. Without legal experience—specifically litigation experience—this is no easy task.

> *A primary difference between a trained lawyer and a self-represented litigant is the ability of a seasoned litigator to present a case that is easy-to-understand, inclusive of all legally relevant details and compelling."*

The list of obstacles threatening self-represented litigants would not be complete without acknowledging the hurdles associated with navigating the civil justice system while managing the other aspects of life. Civil litigation is a unique specialty that requires a combination of an abundance of time and a set of skills that aren't required in most professions. Few people in our society have the time required to become a self-taught and effective litigator—not to mention the skills required to make efficient use of that time.

Time to research case law, time to prepare filings and time to schedule and prepare for depositions results in time away from child care, work and other life obligations. When project and time management skills are mentioned as necessary to properly litigate a civil lawsuit, these skills are not only related to the requirements of the lawsuit but also apply to the requirements of life. Additionally, it's a given that the vast majority of self-represented litigants have little to no legal training and, in most cases, limited experience in the country's civil courts. Without legal training, these individuals rely on their own professional skills and educational background to navigate the process. Some self-represented litigants have limited formal education—and may also have limited English-language skills. While other self-represented litigants may have specific skills from their own lives that may apply to litigation—a researcher who can focus on case law or someone who works in marketing with strong writing skills—the depth and breadth of skills required to be a successful litigator is unusual and not often found in a self-represented litigator.

The opposing party—the party represented by an attorney—knows that if they're in opposition to a party not represented by a lawyer they have an unmistakable advantage."

The opposing party—the party represented by an attorney—knows that if they're in opposition to a party not represented by a lawyer they have an unmistakable advantage. The attorney of the opposing party has no obligation to a self-represented litigant—a litigant who is their adversary—to assist in their understanding of the rules and civil procedure. In fact, quite the opposite. Given the lawyer's obligation to their own client, an ethical lawyer will be measured in every interaction with an opposing party representing themselves to minimize any potential mis-understanding and legal liability. The opposing party's lawyer is not the place to seek advice for a self-represented litigant.

As a reminder, the issues at stake in a civil lawsuit vary greatly in terms of the ultimate impact upon the lives of the parties. In some instances, a civil lawsuit is trivial, low stakes and of limited consequence—some lawsuits may even be viewed as unworthy of the court's time. On the other hand, the decision rendered in a civil lawsuit may be of fundamental importance to the individuals involved and may have a long-lasting impact. In some instances, the results may be life-defining. Unsurprisingly, given the bewildering complexity and the potential stakes, many litigants—especially self-represented litigants—may feel dazed, exhausted, nervous and simply overwhelmed by the civil justice process.

Guidance and Resources Available for Self-Represented Litigants

As the dynamics of self-represented litigants play out in more than 15,000 civil courts in state, county and municipal jurisdictions, the challenge facing each of the individual litigants who have chosen—or been forced—to represent themselves is one of preparation and execution. How can a self-represented litigant leverage their participation within the civil courts to achieve a positive resolution when the barriers and challenges facing self-represented litigants are so daunting and discouraging?

A constructive first step—a step you've already taken—is to read this book. Understanding the general framework of the civil justice process will help you avoid the appearance and, potentially, the negative consequences that can occur when a judge determines that a litigant—particularly a self-represented litigant—is not prepared and is wasting the court's time. The fastest way to get an unfavorable outcome—such as a dismissed case as a plaintiff or a ruling for the opposition as a defendant—is to demonstrate that you're not respecting the time allotted by the court and—by extension—your case does not deserve a hearing.

This book will help you develop an understanding of the civil justice process and can be a valuable resource as you manage your lawsuit but—given the complexity of civil law—you'll also need to identify and use other sources of information and guidance that can provide assistance related to the norms and practices within the specific court where your case is being heard. The rules of civil procedure are the same in each of the nation's more than 15,000 civil courts but the method of shepherding each case through the process can vary from court to court.

An invaluable resource to learn about the mechanics of local courts are the self-help centers that are becoming increasingly important as the number and percentage of self-represented litigants continues to climb. Each state has a self-help center—in many cases specific counties or municipalities also have self-help centers—designed specifically to assist in legal matters in their respective courts. The self-help center is a good place to find information related to a wide variety of the components that comprise civil courts and civil litigation including the following: information related to specific areas of the law, the rules of procedure specific to the local court, the fee schedule for court activities, the required forms for specific court activities—often including forms related to specific areas of the law—online services such as fee payment and e-filing, information and referrals for relevant legal help and general information related to court operations. The help provided by self-help centers—also referred to as court assistance offices—may include online videos, online articles and documents related to specific, common areas of legal dispute and available via call center assistance, online chat or in-person help depending on the self-help center.

As evident by the scope of the services offered by civil self-help centers, the nation's civil self-help centers are a wealth of invaluable information. Yet, it's important to acknowledge the limitations. Not all civil self-help centers are created equally in terms of both the scope of services offered and the number of self-represented litigants that the individual self-help centers can assist. This is primarily a result of funding. As previously discussed, funding to enable citizens seeking to exercise their civil rights in the civil court system is in short supply. This dynamic applies to civil self-help centers as well. As a result, unfortunately many self-help centers are not sufficiently funded to ensure they have the staff and resources sufficient to meet the demand for their services. The good news is that—while a county or municipality may not all have easy-to-use and accessible self-help centers—most states have online and in-person self-help centers prepared to provide service to self-represented litigants.

Another important consideration when interacting with civil self-help centers is the limitations that govern the operations of self-help centers. Self-help centers are limited in the type of information and guidance they're legally allowed to provide. The staff of self-help centers—generally employed by the court—are restricted from providing legal advice or conducting legal research on behalf of individuals seeking guidance. Additionally, seeking advice from a self-help center staff member does not create an attorney-client relationship and, as a result, any information shared with staff members can not be guaranteed to be held in confidence. In fact, staff members are required to act as a neutral party and can even offer information and guidance to the opposition party if that party seeks help from the same self-help center.

In short, self-help center staff can provide self-represented litigants a wide variety of information and guidance primarily related to how the courts work and not related to what the litigant should do. For example, a self-help center can provide guidance related to completing and filing a form or explain how a given civil procedure works but is restricted from advising on whether or not filling the particular form is the best strategic, legal decision for advancing your case.

The intent behind this book is to serve as a resource in combination with the information and guidance provided by civil self-help centers. This book provides readers with an overview of the civil justice process and the self-help centers offer tactical and operational guidance related to the mechanics of civil justice.

As a self-represented litigant, it's important to appreciate how difficult winning in a civil court is and understand the importance of seeking any advantage or advice that may assist in advancing—and ultimately winning—your case. Unfortunately, the judge presiding over the case is unlikely to be a source of advice for a self-represented litigant. Judges are required to act as neutral parties and bound by law to ensure self-represented litigants adhere to the same standards as licensed, practicing lawyers. The judge may be more, or less, tolerant of the mistakes of a self-represented litigant—this can vary greatly depending on the judge. A judge may provide a self-represented litigant with direction or instruction but will always stop short of advocating for a self-represented litigant. In civil court, the judge is there to administer justice—not assist a self-represented litigant through the process. The judge is a critical actor in the drama that is civil litigation, but the judge is not a viable source for help for a self-represented litigant.

Another path worth exploring as a self-represented litigant is establishing a relationship with an attorney via an unbundled legal services agreement. The unbundling of legal services has emerged as a viable alternative to the full-service delivery of legal services with benefits to both clients and attorneys—and another path to, potentially, assist a self-represented litigant in securing insight that may mean the difference between a successful and unsuccessful legal experience. The increase in the number of self-represented litigants and the cost associated with full-service legal representation—meaning traditional legal representation from the filing of a complaint to the resolution of a complaint—have led to the legal industry to adopt an approach that allows clients to engage with lawyers on a limited basis.

Unbundling is most often offered with regard to procedural matters—such as providing simple advice and guidance, explaining the procedures required for a given legal activity, filing the proper documents with the court such as complaints or pleadings, serving or disclosing documents to the opposing party or relevant third parties, interpreting court documentation or—in some instances—appearing in court for a limited scope hearing. It's critical to understand that the delivery of unbundled legal services—in most cases—does not constitute the establishment of an attorney-client relationship. In other words, the client remains a self-represented litigant from the perspective of the court and the attorney assumes no liability related to the outcome of the case (a fact that's, in most cases, made explicit by an engagement letter signed prior to the delivery of unbundled legal services).

The goal of unbundled legal services is to provide a level of legal guidance from an attorney to a self-represented litigant with the understanding that the self-represented litigant will proceed with the actions required of the case without the assistance of the lawyer. Unbundled legal services are inherently limited in scope (in fact, some folks refer to this approach as limited scope representation) designed to equip the self-represented litigant with the knowledge required to proceed with the case.

The concept of unbundled legal services was initially introduced in the legal profession in the early 2000's based on the assumption that self-represented litigants will be better served with some degree of professional guidance—rather than the previous approach which either required litigants to self-represent or hire an attorney for full representation. Unbundled legal services is also designed to assist the legal market by enabling more litigants to have access to legal expertise in a market with a limited supply of lawyers. Depending on the facts and circumstances of your case and your own level of comfort with navigating the civil justice system, obtaining advice and guidance from an attorney in an unbundled arrangement may be a worthwhile path to investigate. Unbundled legal services are a cost-effective option for many self-represented litigants who either don't want to fund—or can't afford to fund—a lawyer in the traditional sense of full representation. Of course, this type of partial representation has pros and cons as well as proponents and critics.

Proponents of unbundled legal services contend that the approach enables more litigants to benefit from the guidance of a legal expert in a cost-effective manner than the previous dichotomy of full legal representation or self-representation. This is particularly helpful in a legal market where demand for legal services far exceeds the number of available attorneys and the time required for an attorney to properly serve all litigants.

Critics of unbundled legal services[1] state that the strengths associated with the approach are outweighed by the fact that the self-represented litigant is still responsible—solely responsible—for executing the most challenging aspects of the legal process. Gathering evidence via the discovery process, responding to the opposing party's discovery requests, properly interviewing witnesses during a deposition or trial, conducting efficient and effective legal research including gathering case law relevant to the matter at hand and—most importantly—synthesizing all the available information into a compelling argument in preparation for settlement negotiations or trial are the most challenging components of civil litigation. In an unbundled services agreement with an attorney, the self-repre-

---

[1] https://www.law.georgetown.edu/poverty-journal/wp-content/uploads/sites/25/2020/06/01-Cerniglia_Final_Proof.pdf

sented litigant remains responsible for the myriad of tasks that comprise each of these litigation activities.

A self-represented litigant needs to balance the advantages and disadvantages of interacting with an attorney in unbundled legal services arrangements. An effective self-represented litigant can benefit from such a relationship by gaining the type of short-term insight typically offered in such an arrangement while always considering, and questioning, the impact of the short-term action with the long-term, legal strategy. In this way, a self-represented litigant can use the insight gained from an attorney to advance their case incrementally while positioning themselves to ultimately achieve the goal of winning the lawsuit. This combination of strategic thinking and tactical action is the same approach a legally-trained attorney would adopt to develop a winning argument—and the same approach a self-represented litigant should seek to emulate. As stated previously, a wise litigator seeks to leverage every avenue to gain an advantage in civil litigation—interacting with a legal expert, even on a limited basis, certainly seems like an avenue worth exploring for a savvy self-represented litigant.

The Frivolity of the Frivolous Lawsuit Argument

"Laws are spider webs through which the big flies pass and the little ones get caught."

— HONORE DE BALZAC

Any casual observer of this country's political discourse is familiar with the phrases "frivolous lawsuit" and "tort reform." A slew of seemingly egregious lawsuits have gained the media's attention and, by extension, the public's incredulity and become exhibits for the dysfunctional nature of the civil justice system. Politicians and political action committees leverage these outrageous tales as justification to alter the rules and guidelines of the civil courts. This may seem like just another area of political disagreement in a polarized country but the debate does have a foundation in the law.

The term "frivolous lawsuit" has a legal definition and penalties exist to prevent the filing of complaints considered frivolous due to their lack of "legal merit." A litigant's complaint may be considered frivolous if it is not supported by the underlying evidence and can't possibly meet the standards of the complaint. The true test to determine if a lawsuit is frivolous is if the complaint is not supported by the state's established case law and can't reasonably expect the case to serve as legal precedent and change the case law. In layman's terms, a lawsuit is frivolous if the plaintiff can't reasonably expect to win and the intention of the complaint is not to win but harass and/or delay.

The same legal concept can also be applied to an individual legal motion or an appeal of a judge's ruling on a motion or case. If the opposing party can successfully argue that a motion was filed for the sole purpose of harassing the other party or delaying the proceedings, that motion can be deemed frivolous. A judge, in a higher court, can also deem an appeal of the preceding court proceedings—either a motion or a case ruling—as frivolous if the appeal lacks a component that is reviewable from a legal perspective.

Advocates for tort reform contend that the current civil court system is overwhelmed with lawsuits that lack legal merit. Tort reform proponents assert that contingent fee agreements between attorneys and clients fuel the filing of frivolous lawsuits as lawyers seek punitive damage awards that far exceed the actual damage inflicted upon their client. According to tort reform advocates, the contingent fee arrangement—typically structured to award lawyers with a 33 percent share of the damages recovered—provides an incentive for litigating attorneys to pursue potentially meritless complaints in pursuit of significant paydays. An additional complaint often expressed by tort reform advocates is the fact that trial lawyers receive an unfair percentage of monetary damages when compared to their clients who were actually damaged by the other party.

To rectify this situation, tort reformers offer a wide variety of modifications including reducing the statute of limitations for certain claims, limitations on venues available for certain complaints, limits on contingency fee arrangements, the institution of punitive damage award caps, the establishment of non-economic damage award caps (such as monetary awards in medical malpractice lawsuits associated with medical harm as opposed to monetary harm), and the adoption of the "English rule" which requires the losing party to automatically pay the attorney's fees of the prevailing party.

The commonality among the proposed reforms advocated by tort reform proponents is the impact each would have in limiting the ability and opportunity of potential litigants to exercise their rights in the civil courts. The stated intention of reform advocates is to alleviate the burden, from both financial and time perspectives, imposed upon the civil courts by frivolous lawsuits. The actual effect would be a methodical and deliberate reduction of citizens' ability to rely upon the civil courts to seek restitution and justice. By examining the effects of each proposed reform individually, the cumulative result—the desired result—becomes evident:

- Reducing the statute of limitations for certain complaints would decrease the number of lawsuits filed with the civil courts. Yet, this curtailment would be indiscriminate. Both frivolous and valid complaints may be time barred as a result of such changes. The result may be a reduction in frivolous lawsuits filed with the court, but the cost would be an increase in valid complaints, and potentially justified litigants, not having their day in court.
- Imposing venue limitation would have a similar impact as a reduction in the statute of limitations—a sweeping outcome that doesn't distinguish between frivolous and meritorious lawsuits.
- A restriction on contingency fee arrangements between an attorney and their clients (or clients in the case of class action lawsuits) is the issue most debated in the tort reform discussion. Advocates of reform criticize the incentive structure that guides attorneys and the percentage of settlements or judgments that become income to the lawyers, rather than damages to the litigants. Opponents against contingency fee restrictions contend that the financial incentives available to attorneys as a result of contingency fee arrangements are required to ensure valid complaints are represented and litigants are able

to pursue their day in court. This is particularly true of plaintiffs that are unable to fund their case from the beginning and are only able to pursue a lawsuit via a contingency fee arrangement.

- The institution of punitive damages and non-economic damage award caps would not limit the filing of frivolous lawsuits. It would only result in limiting the financial liability of defendants in the event the plaintiff prevails. This reform would essentially protect the defendant, but would not address the issue of overwhelmed courts that tort reform advocates state is their primary concern.

- The "English rule" states that the defeated party is held responsible for the attorney's fees of both parties. Opponents of the adoption of the "English rule" cite the potential chilling effect that could occur. Filing a lawsuit is already a daunting affair. If a plaintiff understood they'd be held responsible for the opposing party's legal fees if they did not prevail, the "English rule" may provide a disincentive that would prevent many plaintiffs from pursuing justice in the civil courts.

When evaluating the necessity of the proposed tort reforms, the existing rules and procedures already codified to prevent the filing of frivolous lawsuits need to be considered.

In any civil case, the defense attorney has an opportunity to petition the court to dismiss the case on the grounds that the complaint has no legal merit, or in other words, is frivolous. If the judge agrees, the case can be dismissed and the judge can even impose sanctions upon the plaintiff's attorney. The motion to dismiss is generally filed by the defense attorney at the inception of the case—essentially stating that the plaintiff can't possibly meet their legal burden and the case should not consume more of the court's time.

The motion for summary administration is another tool utilized to prevent the burden placed upon the court by frivolous lawsuits. This motion is generally deployed after the case has been filed and some evidence has been presented to the court. By filing a motion for summary administration, the attorney is requesting that the judge examine the facts already presented and conclude that—given the facts and circumstances as understood at that point in time—the opposition can't possibly win and further court proceedings are unnecessary.

> ❝❝ *The stated intention of reform advocates is to alleviate the burden, from both financial and time perspectives, imposed upon the civil courts by frivolous lawsuits. The actual effect would be a methodical and deliberate reduction of citizens' ability to rely upon the civil courts to seek restitution and justice.*"

A third strategy commonly deployed in legal proceedings is the motion for attorney's fees. The "English rule" requires the losing party to pay each side's attorney's fees *automatically*. The motion for attorney's fees, when filed on behalf of the defendant, is essentially stating that the lawsuit should never have been filed—the lawsuit was frivolous—and the plaintiff should be responsible for the defendant's attorney's fees. This motion differs from the "English rule" in that the motion needs to be filed and considered by a judge—the judge does not automatically award attorney's fees. The judge may rule that the lawsuit had merit, but the plaintiff never met its burden of proof—considerations not examined under the "English rule."

Additionally, state bar associations require licensed attorneys to comply with ethics rules governing frivolous lawsuits. Attorneys who fail to comply can be sanctioned and the bar association may publish specifics regarding cases and ethical lapses by attorneys that violate ethics rules, including rules and procedures related to the filing of frivolous lawsuits.

The reforms referenced in this book are the linchpins of the tort reform movement. These considerations are the basis for the foundation of entire political action committees—such as the American Tort Reform Association—and the primary talking points—and areas of disagreement—when the dysfunction of the American civil justice system receives media coverage. Yet, time-proven rules and procedures for limiting frivolous lawsuits have been available in civil legal practice for decades.

The time and money required to exercise your legal rights by filing a lawsuit in the civil courts are, for many citizens, prohibitive. Given the sheer volume of lawsuits filed each year in the United States, there are guaranteed to be lawsuits filed with little to no merit. Yet, the vast majority of lawsuits are filed as a result of a true hardship that may or may not be actionable in the civil courts. Funding a lawsuit is difficult. Dedicating the necessary time and energy to a lawsuit is difficult. Finding a lawyer—much less a lawyer willing to work on contingency—is difficult. Yet, the impact of the reforms advocated by the tort reform would be to limit citizens' access to the civil courts and make pursuing justice an even more daunting task than it already is. That's the frivolity of the frivolous lawsuit argument. That's the frivolity of the tort reform movement.

Introduction to the Civil Justice System

"The law is so complex and voluminous that no one, not even the most knowledgeable lawyer, can understand it all. Moreover, lawyers and legal scholars have not gone out of their way to make the law accessible to the ordinary person. Just the opposite: Legal professionals, like the priests of some obscure religion, too often try to keep the law mysterious and inaccessible."

— JAY FEINMAN (ATTORNEY AND AUTHOR OF *DELAY, DENY, DEFEND: WHY INSURANCE COMPANIES DON'T PAY CLAIMS AND WHAT YOU CAN DO ABOUT IT*)

When confronted by the need to participate in the civil justice system—either by choice as a plaintiff or by necessity as a defendant—the initial reaction is most often distorted by emotion. This is an understandable and essentially human reaction. A plaintiff files a lawsuit to rectify an injustice; or, at least, a perceived injustice. On the other hand, a defendant may be surprised. This initial reaction will be combined with disbelief (at the prospect of being unjustly accused), uneasiness (at the prospect of being caught) or, potentially, some combination of the two. This same dynamic can be applied to complex, multi-million–dollar estate lawsuits and relatively small dollar amount actions, so-called "nuisance" lawsuits. Every lawyer in the country can regale you with stories of individuals who've spent $10,000 to recover $1,000. Emotional decision-making is the only explanation for such behavior.

It's difficult to make decisions on a purely rational basis when embroiled in an inherently emotional and adversarial situation. Instead of focusing on the facts and events that reinforce a participant's existing narrative, a savvy litigant will weigh the value of all available evidence—or lack of evidence—and consider the opposing party's perspective and strategic options. The success of any legal action is based on the ability to perform honest and effective cost-benefit analysis as a means of deciding the next, rational chess move despite the difficult-to-resist temptation to react emotionally rather than prepare purposefully.

> *Every lawyer in the country can regale you with stories of individuals who've spent $10,000 to recover $1,000."*

The first decision, on behalf of the plaintiff, is to decide if the facts and circumstances support the filing of a legal complaint. To properly assess the viability of a legal action, the first two factors a potential plaintiff needs to consider are cause and damages. In other words, did the potential defendant cause harm to the plaintiff and, if so, what were the monetary damages to the plaintiff as a result of the defendant's actions?

The key phrase is *monetary damages*. The entirety of the civil justice system is designed to rectify financial damages inflicted by one party upon another. This is the primary difference between the civil justice system and the criminal justice system. Of course, there are times when the two court systems overlap or when the circumstances of a specific situation necessitate the involvement of individuals from both court systems.

To avoid confusion, one simple way of understanding the difference between the civil and criminal justice systems is to consider the participants and the potential outcomes. In a civil proceeding, the participants are generally individuals, groups of individuals, companies, non-profit organizations. The dispute in civil court concerns financial harm and, as a result, the desired remedy in the form of an award of monetary damages. In criminal court, one of the parties is a city, state, or federal agency acting on behalf of the victim(s) in prosecuting the alleged perpetrator. In this case, the victim is a witness—often, the most important witness—but not a party to the proceedings. The result of a criminal proceeding may be a variety of punishments for the perpetrator's bad actions including fines, jail time, and criminal restitution (financial compensation to the victim). It's important to keep in mind that the civil court system is the best venue for the pursuit of monetary damages—as this is the primary purpose of the civil court system, in contrast to the criminal courts. Restitution is not the primary goal of a criminal proceeding and, most importantly, the amount of damages in the form of both compensatory and punitive awards will generally be significantly greater in civil court—particularly when one considers the parameters regarding restitution associated with criminal actions. In short, a good rule of thumb is any monetary damage due to the victim of a criminal act is best recovered in civil court where the victim will be a plaintiff in a civil suit—rather than a witness in a criminal suit.

> *The entirety of the civil justice system is designed to rectify financial damages inflicted by one party upon another. This is the primary difference between the civil justice system and the criminal justice system."*

Cause and damages are the foundation of any civil action and the basis for evaluating the facts and circumstances of any case. To understand the likelihood of success for a possible lawsuit—or the risk facing a defendant once a lawsuit has been filed—an examination of the specific complaint filed with the civil court, the legal elements of that complaint, and the burden of proof to successfully prove the plaintiff's cause of action is required.

The legal elements of a complaint provide the guidance required by the court to consider a wide variety of cases—each with its unique set of variables—and, ideally, produce a fair and equitable resolution for each party. The elements of a complaint enable the participants to discern the critical distinction between a bad action and an illegal action. It's tempting to consider an action unfair, unjust or, even, morally objectionable and assume the civil court system will, obviously, view this action with the same lens. The elements of a complaint—combined with the state's existing case law—provide the litigants with direction and reduce ambiguity when considering a plaintiff or defendant's legal position and likelihood for successful resolution. Of course, the law is inherently subject to interpretation. In addition to discrediting the set of facts your attorney seeks to introduce, the opposing counsel will also present the court with a different interpretation of the same facts—often presented as arguments "in the alternative"—to propose a different narrative that either degrades your version of events or strengthens their own case.

The next consideration is the statute of limitations for the complaint. This simply translates into the time period allowed to file a complaint from the time the cause of damages occurred. On the surface, this concept is fairly straightforward and often utilized by a defendant's attorney to prevent a lawsuit from being filed or ensure the lawsuit is immediately dismissed. In practice, the statute of limitations provisions in some areas of the law are highly reliant upon a number of variables and can be subject to interpretation. For example, in cases of breach of fiduciary duty—a highly specialized area of estate and trust law—a requirement of a trustee with a fiduciary duty to a beneficiary is to provide annual accounting for an irrevocable trust. Failing to do so is considered a breach of fiduciary duty—in other words, a breach of the contract between trustee and beneficiary. In this example, the statute of limitations for filing a lawsuit against the trustee by a qualified beneficiary is four years in the state of Florida but, critically, the statute of limitations clock does not begin to toll until a full and complete accounting has been provided to the beneficiary. In other words, the trustee could be successfully sued many years after the failure to provide an accounting—many years beyond the four chronological years—if the beneficiary successfully argues that the clock did not begin to toll regarding the four-year statute of limitations due to the trustee's failure to provide a full and complete accounting.

The purpose of this examination of the legal concept of statute of limitations is to simply raise awareness that a seemingly expired statute of limitations does not necessarily signify an inability for a plaintiff to file a complaint. This is a great example of the complexity and nuance that is so prevalent throughout the civil justice system. A plaintiff may be able to devise an argument that convinces the court that the complaint is not time barred. Also, the statute of limitations differs by complaint. As a result, it's important to investigate and evaluate each potential complaint for your specific situation, and the various time restrictions, as defined by the applicable state's legal code. Of course, the same concepts hold true for potential defendants weighing their potential liability related to a legal matter.

In order to prevail in a lawsuit, the plaintiff is required to produce evidence that supports the elements of the complaint filed with the court. For example, if the plaintiff alleges that a breach of contract occurred the plaintiff would need to produce documentation that a contract was, in fact, entered by the two parties *and* evidence that one party failed to fulfill their commitment regarding the contract. In the absence of evidence of a contract, the plaintiff will not have standing to sue. Without evidence that supports the allegation that a breach of contract occurred, the plaintiff will not have a valid complaint.

In the above situation, this assumes the burden of proof—in legal terms, a preponderance of the evidence—rests with the plaintiff. In other words, the plaintiff needs to prove to the court that a contractual relationship between the two parties has been established and the contract was violated. In this common legal scenario, the defendant does not have a burden—they don't have to produce any evidence justifying their standing or their case to the judge. They simply have to refute the evidence introduced to the court by the plaintiff. There are situations when the burden of proof shifts from plaintiff to defendant. In the example referenced earlier regarding breach of fiduciary duty between a trustee and a beneficiary, the trustee is required to provide annual accounting of a trust's assets to a beneficiary. The burden in this example rests with the trustee—potentially, the defendant in a breach of fiduciary duty lawsuit—to prove that the trustee complied with the requirement and delivered the required accounting to the beneficiary.

Meeting the burden of proof standards is often accomplished in a legal proceeding via the discovery process. In the best possible situation, the plaintiff already has the evidence required to win their case. More likely, the plaintiff has some evidence—or at least an understanding that a bad act occurred—and requires other documentation to prove their assertions. In this case, the discovery process is utilized to ensure the opposing party or a third party is compelled by the court to produce the evidence requested by the plaintiff. The discovery process may not feature the theatrics often associated with courtroom drama, but it's often the most important component of a legal proceeding. The ability to ask the right question and uncover the required evidence needed to prove a plaintiff's complaint within the discovery process can often mean the difference between a successful or failed lawsuit.

Yet, the discovery process can only be utilized after a lawsuit has been filed. There's a cost in filing a lawsuit—legal proceedings are expensive and require significant time commitments.

Additionally, once a lawsuit has been filed a plaintiff is at risk of being sued by the defendant to recover the defendant's legal fees if the defendant can prove the lawsuit filed by the plaintiff is frivolous.

This raises the critical question of legal strategy of determining the best time to file a lawsuit. Ideally, a lawsuit isn't filed until the plaintiff has already obtained all necessary evidence required to support their argument. Of course, this isn't always plausible or realistic—hence, the discovery process. As an alternative to the discovery process, it's often worth considering methods of obtaining information—potentially, public information from third parties—to bolster a plaintiff's case prior to filing a lawsuit. Adopting an evidence-gathering approach outside the bounds of a lawsuit eliminates the risk of being sued as a plaintiff for the defendant's legal fees, enables the plaintiff to bolster the strength of their case and, as a result, gain a deeper understanding of the potential situation and determine the best possible complaint to file with the legal elements the plaintiff's evidence supports.

> " The discovery process may not feature the theatrics often associated with courtroom drama, but it's often the most important component of a legal proceeding."

If the decision is made by a plaintiff to file a lawsuit, consistently maintaining focus on the goals of the lawsuit and the evidence required to meet the burden of proof is the best method for ensuring a successful resolution while minimizing costs. The following concepts can provide guidance to a plaintiff in a process that can be extremely complex—and, at times, intentionally complicated by the defendant in order to refute the plaintiff's ability to obtain evidence and meet their burden of proof:

- Review all available evidence already in your possession.
- Explore all possible complaints available within the civil code to resolve the issue—in essence, determine the basis of your lawsuit—by examining the available evidence.
- Understand the legal elements associated with each unique complaint and the pros and cons—from a legal element perspective—of pursuing each potential complaint.
- Identify the evidence required to meet the elements of the complaints under consideration and determine a plan to obtain any required evidence not currently in your possession.

For a defendant, scrutinizing the plaintiff's goals and the various legal strategies available can provide guidance as the defendant seeks to refute the plaintiff's complaint.

An Overview of the Civil Justice System

"The legal system is often a mystery, and we, its priests, preside over rituals baffling to everyday citizens."

— HENRY MILLER

The decision to file a legal complaint, or the requirement to defend against a filed lawsuit, can be intimidating to individuals not already acquainted with the law and the civil court system. Despite the fact that the involvement in a legal action is a significant event in life—in some instances, one of life's defining events—I've assembled some statistics below to convey the fact that millions of individuals every year find themselves as participants in the civil legal system and litigants in the courts. See below for statistics sourced from the American Bar Association and the Court Statistics Project that convey the size and scope of the civil legal system in the United States.

The Court Statistics Project[1]—a joint effort by the National Center for State Courts (NCSC) and the Conference of State Court Administrators (COSCA)—is dedicated to the collection and interpretation of court-related data in the United States. This organization provides invaluable insight detailing the operations of the civil and criminal legal systems.

According to the Court Statistics Project, 95 percent of U.S. cases are filed in state courts—as opposed to federal courts.

---

[1] https://www.courtstatistics.org

Data regarding civil filings in federal court can be found here[1]. With this in mind, if you're a litigant in a lawsuit in the United States in most instances your case will be heard in one of the state's courts.

As demonstrated by the latest available data, the majority of states in the U.S. have experienced a recent increase in civil case filings in 2018 compared to the previous two years. This indicates a resurgence in civil caseloads compared to the number of civil lawsuits filed in state courts in the preceding decade. The Court Statistics Project has been publishing court caseload statistics since 1975 but has yet to release their analysis for recent years.

There are many reasons for the yearly changes in civil case filings, but what is constant is that the total number of civil cases filed annually in state courts easily exceeds 15 million. The constant litigation also provides steady employment for attorneys who specialize in civil law disputes. According to the American Bar Association, in 2018 there were 1,338,678 licensed and active attorneys practicing law in the United States.

If you're considering filing a civil lawsuit, know that you have plenty of company as a litigant. There are plenty of lawyers to assist with your effort but, increasingly, individuals are choosing to represent themselves in civil court due to a variety of factors—particularly the cost associated with engaging legal representation as detailed below.

When considering the types of cases filed in state civil courts, the Court Statistics Project[2] examined the civil caseload in twenty-seven states in 2018. This analysis segmented civil caseloads into seven distinct categories including the following:

---

[1] https://www.uscourts.gov/statistics-reports/judicial-business-2018

[2] https://www.courtstatistics.org/__data/assets/pdf_file/0014/40820/2018-Digest.pdf

- Contract
- Small claims
- Probate/estate
- Tort
- Mental health
- Real property
- Other civil cases

The data indicates that forty-seven percent, nearly half, of civil cases are related to contract disputes when considering caseload in aggregate for the twenty-seven states. Small claims cases, which are the second-most common type of civil lawsuit, accounted for an additional seventeen percent of the civil cases in the twenty-seven states examined. The combination of contract lawsuits and small claims lawsuits, which often have a contractual component related to the dispute, contribute more than half of the civil caseload in twenty-one of the twenty-seven states examined and more than two-thirds of the civil caseload in twelve of the twenty-seven states considered.

Yet, when considering the sheer volume of civil cases filed in the United States, even smaller categories of civil cases—for example, real estate disputes—represent millions of lawsuits filed every year in the United States.

The Court Statistics Project's 2018 study of state court filings also provides information regarding trends within the four most common types of civil lawsuits: contracts, small claims, probate/estate and tort. The combination of civil cases in the relevant—and most common—areas of civil law represent over eighty percent of civil cases filed in the United States. The primary insight is that, in each of the four areas of civil law examined, the trends demonstrate an increase in overall caseload as well as an increase in each area of the law individually. If you're a potential litigant, the study performed by the Court Statistics Project reinforces the message that there are huge numbers of your fellow citizens availing themselves of the civil court system.

Last, and in some respects most importantly, the Court Statistics Project completed a study to estimate the typical costs of litigation by the different types of cases most often filed in civil courts. The study completed in 2013 titled "Estimating the Cost of Civil Litigation" details the median cost of different types of civil cases including an estimation of costs as it relates to the various stages within a civil case. It's important to remember that each case is individual and unique—as such the facts and circumstances of your case will dictate the required legal effort and costs. Yet, the graph provides important context for the costs associated with some of the most commonly filed civil lawsuits. The study demonstrated that the median cost for a case related to an automobile accident was $43,000, the median cost to litigate a premises liability case was $54,000, the median cost of a real property case was $66,000, the median cost of employment-related litigation was $88,000 and the median cost of a case litigated a contract dispute was $91,000. The Court Statistic Project study also provides median cost data related to the various stages of litigation for each of the types of civil cases examined including costs associated with lawsuit initiation, discovery, pre-trial and trial activities, settlement, post-disposition activities and total costs.

The statistics convey a portion of the narrative but, when considering your own case, it's important to consider your specific circumstances within the parameters of the types of cases—contracts, small claims, probate, and tort—and the unifying characteristics of each area of the law. When considering the likelihood of success in the civil justice arena, the potential return-on-investment, the ability to conduct discovery and obtain evidence, the complexity of the legal issues, and the individuals and personalities involved in the legal proceeding should all be considered when evaluating the strength of your case.

For example, many small claims cases are centered on issues that are fairly simple to understand and don't require extensive legal analysis or expertise. Of course, small claims cases inherently have a limited return-on-investment which may make the pursuit of the issue via a legal remedy unattractive given the potential expense required compared to the total potential damages available. This dynamic has resulted in small claims cases as an area of the law where litigants have increasingly decided to represent themselves.

Tort law, which is essentially a category of the countless ways one party can harm another party, presents litigants with a seemingly endless set of possibilities and—confusingly—case law that may or may not apply to your particular circumstances. A common challenge with a tort complaint is to understand how common it is to resolve this type of issue within the confines of the civil justice process. Is there case law that directly addresses the issue(s) at stake? What would the opposing party argue with regard to your interpretation of the case law (in other words, are you sure there is case law that specifically addresses your circumstances?)? And, as always, how does the anticipated cost of the tort complaint compare to the potential damages if the lawsuit is successful?

Contract law is unique in that this area of the law is highly reliant on documentation and, critically, the legal interpretation of the relevant documents. Does a contract exist between the two parties and, if so, what is stated in the agreement? This area of the law often demands skilled, and likely expensive, legal representation as the crux of each case is focused on devising the intent of the contract language and proving that intent—either via supporting documentation and statements or case law demonstrating similar situations (ideally both). A situation that, on the surface, appears to be glaringly obvious can evolve into a morass of legal opinion and minutiae—expensive minutiae—that may alter the return-on-investment calculation.

Finally, probate, trust, and estate litigation is essentially a form of contract law that requires the interpretation of important documents at a time of heightened emotions. Often, the litigants involve different family members attempting to clarify the intent of the estate documents—the wishes of the deceased—in a legal forum that isn't conducive to restraint and reasonable compromise. Given the notorious nuance and complexity involved in estate law, this is a recipe for hefty legal bills. It's critical to understand the potential damages at stake—in other words, the financial net worth of the deceased—and your own *legal binding* claim to an inheritance when involved in estate litigation.

As you consider your own potential litigation, the statistics above can help place into context your own situation. Understanding the court's caseload, the types of litigation most often filed within civil courts and the average cost of the specific area of litigation of your lawsuit provide helpful guardrails as you consider the parameters of your own case and the likelihood that you'll prevail in court.

Legal Parties and Participants

Every Character Plays Their Role

"All the world's a stage."

— WILLIAM SHAKESPEARE, *AS YOU LIKE IT*

Regardless of the complexity of the controversy, the issues being litigated, or the potential damages at stake, a number of commonalities exist with every single civil lawsuit filed in the United States. Each legal action requires a plaintiff who initiates the proceedings by filing the lawsuit and a defendant who stands accused of bad actions. Each party may choose to be represented by legal counsel or may choose to represent themselves and every matter has a judge who presides over the proceeding and issues rulings related to issues of fact and law (Note: *pro se* legal representation—the concept of a party representing oneself—is allowed in many instances but, even in those instances, every legal party has representation and the party representing themselves acts in different capacities). Yet, the outcome of any particular legal action is never guaranteed. Of course, different sets of facts and differing interpretations of the law make every case unique but there's another, complex variable that needs to be considered in every legal action: the actions of individual human beings.

Lawsuits are won and lost based on the individual actions of plaintiffs, defendants, their respective lawyers, witnesses, expert witnesses, juries, and—of course—judges. Understanding the different motivations, potentially conflicting incentives, personalities, and experiences—both legal and life—of each participant in any given legal proceeding is vital information when weighing the likely outcome of individual decisions within the course of a lawsuit as well as the potential for success of a given legal strategy. This includes a critical and honest assessment of yourself—as a whole person, not simply a legal party—in terms of your role in the proceedings. With regard to representing yourself in court, a person needs a clear-eyed evaluation of the capabilities required to successfully navigate the civil justice system and their own experience and expertise. The job of legal advocate is a combination of project manager, communicator (both verbal and written), researcher, negotiator and critical thinker. If these are qualities that you have—and skills you exercise in your everyday life—then you may be suited to representing yourself depending on the facts and circumstances of your case. If this limited list of required skills raises concern when you're assessing your own capabilities, you may want to consider hiring legal representation.

> ❝ *Understanding the different motivations, potentially conflicting incentives, personalities, and experiences—both legal and life—of each participant in any given legal proceeding is vital information when weighing the likely outcome of individual decisions within the course of a lawsuit as well as the potential for success of a given legal strategy.*"

From a strictly legal perspective, a party in a lawsuit does not have to be a human being. A business, government entity, activist organization, or trade union—for example—can be plaintiff or defendant in legal proceedings. Additionally, human beings can participate in different capacities beyond their individual capacity. For example, a person may be involved in a lawsuit in their legal capacity as a trustee or in their professional capacity as a lawyer or officer of a company, without their individual capacity being a party to the lawsuit.

The motivations of plaintiffs are as varied as the human condition itself. The desire to fulfill an emotional need—such as the need for closure, an attempt to get attention, or lust for sheer revenge—can explain a plaintiff's actions just as easily as a righteous pursuit of justice. Given the inherent complexity of the human condition, many plaintiffs may have multiple motivations—even motivations in conflict—at the time of the complaint filing. During the course of the lawsuit, these original motivations may wither or harden based on the legal process, the course of life events, and/or the plaintiff's personality. If a person is conflict-averse, and is simply seeking acknowledgment of a wrongdoing or only wants their voice heard, those traits and circumstances may motivate the person to settle the case early. On the other hand, if a person is indignant about an injustice—either perceived or real—and is willing to rearrange the circumstances of their life to seek justice, be prepared for the type of protracted and relentless battle most people imagine when they hear the word *lawsuit*.

Defendants are the same—human beings governed by a wide variety of motivations, personalities, emotions, and previous experiences. A defendant with a lifetime of experience with the legal system, established relationships with a trusted legal team, an understanding of the law, and the financial resources to litigate extensively presents a much more daunting opponent than a first-time defendant reactively scrambling to find legal representation to respond to an unexpected complaint.

The first step in evaluating the likelihood of success for your legal endeavor—whether as plaintiff or defendant—is a thorough and unsparing assessment of the opposing party. The types of questions to consider include the following:

- Is the opposing party an individual? A company? An activist group focused on this specific issue?
- Is the opposing party represented by legal counsel or representing themselves? If the opposing party is representing themselves, are they a licensed attorney? Do they have legal training or deep experience with the civil justice system and—in particular—litigation?
- Does the opposing party have a history of litigation? A better-than-average understanding of the law (as a layperson) or an actual law degree? Established relationships with attorneys who have previously represented the party?
- Does this party's history of litigation include exposure to the specific area of the law that governs the issue of controversy? Or is this legal proceeding an entirely new area of the law that may present difficulties for the opposing party such as a lack of understanding of the details or an inability to leverage existing legal contacts for this complaint?
- If the opposing party is an individual, does this person have a combative personality and is often unwilling to compromise in other areas of life? Or is this person fairly reasonable but, for some as yet unknown reason, has been unwilling to find a mutually agreeable solution to this issue without legal intervention? Understanding that reason is a critical component to resolving the issue—regardless of legal standing and procedures.
- If the opposing party is a corporation, does this entity have a history of settling cases early to avoid legal expenses? Or a reputation for ruthless litigation and need to avoid precedent to forestall a landslide of similar legal complaints from other, potentially impacted parties?
- Does the opposing party have the financial resources to fund a long litigation effort? Or would funding a legal

battle over an extended period of time impact, or even threaten, other areas of the opposing party's life?

It's not always possible to develop a complete understanding of the opposing party's personality, emotional motivations and outlook, financial resources, legal experience, and legal network but a savvy legal client will collect and analyze as much information as possible to inform any legal endeavor both prior to filing the initial complaint and throughout the course of the proceedings.

This level of analysis should not be restricted to the legal parties to a complaint. The next, obvious parties to be examined are the lawyers involved in the action.

The audience for this book is individuals who've decided to self-represent in civil court. Yet, circumstances change, people adjust and—sometimes—you need specific expertise to successfully navigate a complex endeavor such as a civil lawsuit. If you find yourself reconsidering your decision to self-represent, the following insight may be of assistance once you've decided that hiring an experienced attorney is, ultimately, the better decision based on the facts and circumstances of your case.

As a legal client, a thorough examination of the lawyers who may be suited to represent you is required prior to signing an engagement contract. An understanding of the specific area of the law required, experience as a litigator—rather than, for example, a contract attorney who never sees the inside of a courtroom—experience arguing cases with similar issues of controversy and eligibility, and experience within the specific court system where your case will be heard are all critical factors to consider prior to hiring an attorney. As a shrewd client you will also develop a similar understanding of the opposing counsel's skills and experience in order to consider the likelihood of success as well as to compare your own lawyer's background to the competition. Your own lawyer can, likely, provide an assessment of their competition—particularly if both are practicing in a specialized area of the law or practice in a sparsely populated county. Understanding the legal experience, relationships, and personalities of both your own lawyer and opposing counsel may be difficult—particularly for a person without much experience with the law—but there are a number of qualifying questions that can be used to obtain additional insight. Questions such as the following, when applied to both your own lawyer and opposing counsel, can form the basis for such an analysis:

- Do you specialize in the specific area of the law that is relevant to my case? Or does your practice span a number of different specialties?
- How many years of experience do you have in this specific area of the law?
- What percentage of your practice involves actual litigation in a courtroom? How much of your time is spent arguing in a courtroom, conducting depositions, and developing strategies for discovery as opposed to non-litigation legal activities?
- Do you have experience in the specific venue that is relevant for this case? Have you appeared before the judges from this venue? Do you have relationships with these judges based on previous lawsuits and appearances?
- Describe a case from a previous or existing client who you've represented that included a similar set of facts to this case. What are the similarities and differences between this case and your previous similar case load? What are the critical laws, statutes, and procedural considerations that will be relevant in this case?
- Based on the facts as you understand them, what is your strategy for winning this case? What are the biggest weaknesses you see in this case as currently constructed and what is your plan to strengthen those weaknesses?

* What percentage of your practice involves actual litigation in a courtroom? How much of your time is spent arguing in a courtroom, conducting depositions, and developing strategies for discovery as opposed to non-litigation legal activities?"*

Once you have confidence that you've hired the best lawyer to represent you in this particular case or have decided to self-represent—and have an understanding of the opposing counsel's most likely approach and strategy—it's also important to gain insight related to the venue and potential judge who will hear your case. The judge who hears your case has enormous power to influence the outcome of the proceeding—for example, based on their rulings related to the admissibility of evidence. If you're not allowed to obtain, through discovery, the evidence required to make your case or introduce that evidence to the court—your case can be decided by the judge's procedural decisions months or even years before trial. Judges, and the entirety of the legal system, seek to maintain that judges are unbiased arbiters of the law, simply umpires calling balls and strikes. The reality is that judges are human beings with their own biases and opinions based on experiences both inside and outside the courtroom. In unguarded moments, attorneys will divulge that they have favorite judges who are more apt to respect their arguments as well as judges who aren't as favorable—sometimes outright dismissive—to arguments they consider solid law. It's important to understand this context when considering the potential success or failure of your legal endeavor.

Venue is another consideration. If you're filing a lawsuit in a county with judges who have a reputation for ruling favorably or unfavorably in cases that are similar to your own, incorporating that fact into your legal filings—or even deciding to argue for a change of venue—are important considerations within your legal strategy. By understanding your own attorney's personal experience with specific judges and courts—state or federal, district or appellate, for example—you'll have additional facts at your disposal to prepare you for the proceedings.

> *" Describe a case from a previous or existing client who you've represented that included a similar set of facts to this case."*

The strength of the testimony from witnesses, in matters of fact, are obviously critical to the outcome of your case. Yet, it's also important to consider aspects of these individuals' character, presentation, and legal experience when deciding on whether or not to introduce a specific individual to your proceeding. The example often provided in television courtroom dramas is the witness to a crime who is unreliable simply because that person has a criminal record. Yet, the risk of introducing a witness doesn't have to be so dramatic. For example, a witness may not be accustomed to public speaking, or even attention in seemingly high-pressure environments, and—as a result—may get intimidated in a deposition or courtroom. A person may not be the best communicator and, in a high-stakes encounter, may not be the best person to make your case by proxy. Alternatively, a witness may be more polished and experienced than the party of record and a wise attorney may decide to rely more heavily on the testimony of this specific witness than their own client.

A qualified and skilled litigator will be experienced in both identifying personal strengths and weaknesses of witnesses and developing an approach designed to elicit the lawyer's desired outcome in terms of the introduction of favorable facts. Yet, as the client who may have long-standing personal relationships with witnesses as well as the opposing party, your own insight into a witness's personality, communication style, trustworthiness, or any number of characteristics may inform your lawyer's approach. If you're representing yourself, you need to ensure you're able to apply the analytical perspective of a seasoned litigator when you're evaluating the effectiveness of potential witnesses.

The final type of witness who is often deployed during the course of a legal proceeding—particularly a legal proceeding in an area of the law with significant complexity—is the expert witness. This person—whose role is to interpret complex matters of law specifically with regard to the underlying facts of the case—are contracted by one party involved in the litigation in theory to educate the court. In practice, an expert witness is introduced to strengthen the argument of the party who has retained their services—not surprising given the fact that this party is compensating the expert witness for their time. Expert witnesses are subject to cross-examination and—like any other witness—can be leveraged by the opposing party to introduce facts that are not favorable to the party that retained the expert witness. For the purposes of this discussion, it's also important to examine the expert witness—outside the traditional confines of the law and fact basis of the case—to determine if there is an insight that can help you either strengthen or weaken the expert witness. In cases that involve a self-represented litigant, an expert witness can be an effective method of advancing your theory of the case and building credibility with the court.

For example, is the expert witness actually an expert in this area of the law? What are this person's credentials? Experience arguing these complex issues? Do they actually practice in this area of the law or field of expertise or do they generate the bulk of their income serving in this role as expert witness? Does the expert witness have a conflict of interest with either litigant involved in this case?

By considering these questions with respect to an expert witness—or any witness, for that matter—you'll be able to inform your attorney's strategy, particularly with respect to their approach to deposition or court testimony or documentation provided by the expert witness.

As you can see, developing a deeper understanding of all parties involved in litigation is critical to the development of a successful legal strategy. This is an example of how the law is as much art as science. Oftentimes, individuals without extensive legal experience think of legal proceedings as based strictly on the facts and law at issue—yet, it's the interpretation of the relevant facts and case law that determines the outcome of a civil lawsuit. This interpretation is imagined by human beings with their own biases, quirks, and eccentricities. The sooner you understand this fact of human nature, the closer you'll be to successfully resolving your case.

The Search for an Attorney

How to Hire the Best Lawyer for Your Case

"Advice is like snow—the softer it falls, the longer it dwells upon us, and the deeper it sinks into the mind."

— SAMUEL TAYLOR COLERIDGE

If you've already determined that the best course of action is to represent yourself, this section may not be applicable to your situation. On the other hand, if you're weighing the benefits and risks associated with self-representation, engaging with a number of attorneys—in the manner described below—may be a worthwhile investment as you make your decision regarding legal representation. The section below may also be valuable for individuals who previously decided to represent him or herself at the time of the filing of a legal complaint but, given their experiences to date, have determined it may be beneficial to hire an attorney. Be aware that some attorneys may be hesitant to accept a case in which the litigant was originally self-represented due to a variety of concerns including potential mistakes made by the self-represented litigant that may cause issues for the case or the newly hired lawyer. I include this information because circumstances change and individuals who've initially chosen to self-represent may, at some point in the future, decide that hiring an attorney is the best strategy. At that point, the section below may become valuable.

The challenge of imperfect information—in the parlance of economists—is particularly burdensome when considering the need to find the most qualified and appropriate legal representation. In most situations, a potential client has limited, if any, experience within the civil legal market as well as a minimal network of contacts to consult for advice. This typical reality will often combine with the stress and uncertainty resident in most pressure-filled legal circumstances and a sense of urgency to address the situation—either as a potential plaintiff concerned about the potential statute of limitations related to the matter, or a defendant suddenly forced to respond—in a legal setting—to a lawsuit that may have been unexpectedly filed.

Imperfect information is found in most markets for services (and products, for that matter) in our modern economy—in fact, the concept of perfect information is a fiction that only exists in the idealized vision of the economy found in economists' textbooks. Yet, the extenuating circumstances that combine stress and urgency within the legal market—and the overabundance of caution adopted by most law firms—present a problem that leads to confusion, misspent time and money, and—ultimately—inefficient use of both the potential client and lawyer's time when considering the evaluation and hiring process for legal help.

Most clients will only hire an attorney a few times in their lifetime, if that, and typically during a time of heightened stress and turmoil: divorce, custody battles, estate administration after the death of a loved one, the dissolution and failure of a business or business partnership, or an effort to resolve a dispute that couldn't be resolved without legal action. These are the common events that precipitate hiring an attorney. So, we have clients who aren't especially familiar—and certainly not sophisticated—with regard to the complexity associated with the law. These same clients often lack an understanding of the requirements required to address their particular circumstances, never mind the comprehension and legal judgment to evaluate an individual lawyer or law firm's qualifications with respect to the skills and experience required for a successful resolution. As a result, most potential legal customers rely upon the lawyers they contact—lawyers they should be interviewing for a job—as their primary source for information and guidance. This is inherently a conflict as the lawyer—who may or may not want the prospective customer's business based on a variety of factors—will likely tailor their insight to direct a potential client to the conclusion they seek.

Most clients will only hire an attorney a few times in their lifetime, if that, and typically during a time of heightened stress and turmoil: divorce, custody battles, estate administration after the death of a loved one, the dissolution and failure of a business or business partnership, or an effort to resolve a dispute that couldn't be resolved without legal action."

In addition, the legal market as a whole has adopted an industry-wide marketing strategy that lacks transparency, at a minimum, and—in the most egregious cases—willfully restricts the information available to prospective customers. For example, when hiring a lawyer, the basic information a prospective client will be able to obtain include the lawyer's qualifications, the manner in which the lawyer presents him/herself on a website, whether or not the lawyer is currently in good standing with the state bar association, and their hourly rate.

This is a shockingly limited set of facts when considering the potential investment required to fund a robust legal case. With respect to the hourly rate, the only insight this fact communicates is the market's willingness to pay—which is no different than any other service provided in our economy. Yet, lawyers may adjust their rate based on the circumstances or may even adjust their rate based on their desired workload—charging higher rates to enable a lighter case load. This isn't necessarily good or bad—but this information doesn't communicate the individual lawyer's qualifications with regard to the requirements and circumstances of the prospective customer's case.

Qualifications is another area where it's easy for an individual lawyer to present credentials to the marketplace and difficult for the prospective buyer to assess the value of those credentials in terms of their own legal circumstances. An attorney may have attended a well-respected college and law school—an attorney may even be very talented and accomplished in their field—but that doesn't mean that specific attorney is the right person, from requirement-to-qualification and cost-effectiveness perspectives, to represent a prospective client. Of course, that's also not even taking into consideration a phrase my own father often uttered, "even in the best schools, somebody was ranked last in the class."

The next step a prospective client will take is, through web research, a review of law firm websites and a series of discussions to interview lawyers to share the facts and circumstances of their legal predicament and listen to the attorney provide their opinion of the potential case and their insight on the suggested approach to resolution. Remember—attorneys make their living every day making an argument one way or another and most clients aren't properly equipped to identify the flaws in the proposed approach, the missing qualifications the prospective attorney may not have, or even if the lawyers they're interviewing—and I use this word intentionally, but loosely—have the proper, commensurate experience appropriate for their lawsuit. Prospective clients are at risk of being easily overwhelmed by legal jargon, distracted by stories of legal triumphs that may or may not have similarities to their own case—or even be true— and charmed by a lawyer seeking to secure a new client.

Another piece of vetting data used by potential clients in the interview process is confirmation that the attorney is both licensed by the state's bar association and the lawyer is in good standing to practice law. Of course, an attorney who is not licensed or in good standing is immediately disqualified—in fact, a person can't legally practice law if not licensed by the respective state's bar association. Yet, the fact that a prospective attorney is in good standing provides an extremely limited view of the attorney's qualifications for a specific case. Additionally, the statistics support the assertion that it's extremely difficult to be disciplined by the bar and a disbarment is an extraordinary act that is taken only in the most extreme circumstances. A review of the public statistics released by the Florida Bar Association[1] related to attorney discipline reveal that—out of a total population of 108,615 lawyers—forty-two were disbarred and 136 were suspended in 2019 and 2020. Of the forty-two disbarments, only seven were permanent.

Felony conviction of any nature—regardless of whether or not the conviction is related to the legal work of the attorney—or the misuse of a client's funds are the two most common infractions for bar discipline. Information related to past infractions such as disbarment, the revocation of law license, suspensions, and reprimands—can generally be found via the public website of the bar association but the high standard for discipline ensures that all but the most egregious acts are not available to the public as information when deciding to hire an attorney. Given the extraordinary trust required in the attorney-client relationship, the fact that the state bar associations don't provide additional information and guidance related to specific attorneys' patterns and practices—such as a pattern of unethical business practices or, even information unrelated to disciplinary action, such as data regarding their current and historical case load—is a disservice to the public. As a result, the current status of an attorney licensed and in good standing is not useful when considering hiring a specific lawyer.

---

[1] https://www.floridabar.org/public/acap/lawyer-discipline-statistics/

So, how does a potential client evaluate lawyers and law firms prior to signing the retainer agreement and providing the retainer check?

- Understand the law firm, and the specific lawyer's area of specialty, experience within that specialty, and how that expertise and experience align with your own requirements with specific examples of both successes and failures—a person can learn as much (if not more) from losses as victories.
- If you expect a lengthy courtroom battle that requires trial experience, ask about the prospective attorney's typical week or month in terms of actual trial and trial preparation activities compared to other legal work. Do they spend the bulk of their time preparing for and taking depositions? Gathering evidence and synthesizing that evidence into a coherent courtroom narrative? Or is the majority of their time spent outside of an actual courtroom providing contractual legal services? If you think there's a controversy at the core of your case—a dispute that is unlikely to be resolved without significant participation from a judge or jury—you need an attorney who not only claims to be a litigator but also has the day-to-day experience to inform your argument.
- Seek external validation of the law firm and lawyer's credentials. For example, if you're seeking a litigator with a specialty in trust and estate law, contact lawyers with an affiliation with the American College of Trust and Estate Counsel. This is an organization with high standards for membership including contribution to this specialized area of law such as lecturing, writing, teaching, and participating in state bar committees and activities to improve this field of the law. This book contains a list of other legal member groups and associations—in a wide variety of legal specialties—that can be a great resource

to engage with the best attorneys in the area of the law most applicable to your case.

- Many buyers new to the legal market spend time evaluating the pros and cons of hiring a litigator from a large firm compared to a smaller firm when the most enlightening information is gaining an understanding of the business model of the law firm. For example, does the firm focus on the number of transactions executed—most likely measured in the number of settlement agreements executed—or does their business rely on the litigation of fewer—but more complex—cases with inherently larger financial stakes? And, of course, which business model is better aligned to the facts and circumstances of your legal predicament?

The best advice for hiring an attorney—which is similar to general hiring practices of any kind—is to gain an understanding of the lawyer as a person. Why were they attracted to the law as a profession? What was their career vision as they entered law school and how has that changed as their career progressed? What type of cases motivate them—the thrill of solving a previously unsolvable puzzle through the persistent and deliberate accumulation of evidence? The excitement of deposing witnesses and making courtroom arguments? The challenge of the legal arena or the financial windfall from a large settlement?

This line of questioning can be followed by an examination of their historical and current business circumstances, caseload, and related client obligations. For example, one friend of mine hired a divorce attorney who specialized in "no drama" situations—couples divorcing without much in the way of family or financial entanglements. If a person had children or significant joint property, this lawyer wouldn't take the case—he, essentially, built his business around optimizing easy transactions. On the other hand, plenty of law firms who specialize in divorce law actively seek out the most acrimonious situations as a means of maximizing billable hours. Of course, a business model focused on conflict can have its own unexpected consequences. I once met an attorney who—after specializing in estate and trust litigation for years—changed his business model to specialize in the writing of estate documents. From a marketing standpoint, his previous experience allowed him to state that the estate documents he authored were designed to minimize post-death complications but his real motivation was that he wanted to eliminate the constant animosity that was a primary component of his job description as an estate and trust litigator.

In addition to understanding the intrinsic and extrinsic motivations of a potential partner, it's also important to evaluate a prospective lawyer's ability to think logically from the simple perspective of life experience. It's easy as an attorney to focus on the facts and the law. The old adage rings true: if the law is on your side, argue the law, and if the facts are on your side, argue the facts. Of course, great advice but human behavior is unpredictable and—I'd argue—equally as important to the success or failure of a lawsuit. Is the defendant acting guilty? Are they cooperative or obstructive in terms of documentation production? Is every motion met with a bevy of legal objections or are they accepting the rules of civil justice and acting in good faith to resolve a dispute? On the other side of the ledger, is the plaintiff consistent with their set of facts or is there a continual evolution of circumstances to align their complaint with the available facts?

The legal process can bring out the worst in humanity including actions from parties to a lawsuit and their respective legal counsel. As a result, it's easy to explain a person's actions as a result of the legal process itself—but it's important to continue to place these same actions in the context of the original dispute itself. If a party is not acting rationally and logically, is there an underlying reason for this behavior that provides insight into the case? And, most importantly, do you trust the attorney you're considering hiring—or have hired—to separate facts from emotions and leverage insight derived from logical observations of human behavior to help you win your case?

> *" Is the defendant acting guilty? Are they cooperative or obstructive in terms of documentation production? Is every motion met with a bevy of legal objections or are they accepting the rules of civil justice and acting in good faith to resolve a dispute? On the other side of the ledger, is the plaintiff consistent with their set of facts or is there a continual evolution of circumstances to align their complaint with the available facts?"*

Eventually, you have to hire a lawyer (or, if you're a plaintiff, decide not to pursue). The hiring process within the market is fairly standard regardless of the circumstances of the case. Your potential lawyer will first check for conflicts with the opposing party—some lawyers will even perform this verification prior to their initial conversation with a prospective client. The purpose of the conflict check is to ensure the attorney, or the attorney's law firm, does not represent the opposing party. Performing the conflict check is best practice as this avoids any appearance of unethical behavior—if there was never a conversation prior to the conflict check, there's no way the prospective attorney can share any of the details of your case with any party who may have a relationship with the firm and an interest in your case. This is the reason it's recommended that potential new clients avoid sharing details—particularly sensitive information that the potential opposing party may not be privy to—with prospective attorneys. The detailed email with all the facts and circumstances of your case that prospective clients send to a list of the attorneys they think may be interested in accepting their case can land in the inbox of an attorney already representing the opposing side—and, because the prospective client doesn't have a relationship with the attorney—there's no reason why the attorney can't use that email to argue their client's case—even if it's the opposing party.

> ❝ *The detailed email with all the facts and circumstances of your case that prospective clients send to a list of the attorneys they think may be interested in accepting their case can land in the inbox of an attorney already representing the opposing side—and, because the prospective client doesn't have a relationship with the attorney—there's no reason why the attorney can't use that email to argue their client's case—even if it's the opposing party.*"

The conflict check is for the benefit of both the prospective client and the attorney, but keep in mind that the conflict check is intended simply to identify if the law firm is representing the opposing party. The conflict check is not a means of verifying any and all potential conflicts of interest with various parties involved in the case. For example, the conflict check will not bring to any relationship(s) the attorney or law firm may have with potential witnesses involved in the case—who may have influence upon the attorney and a vested interest in the outcome of the case. For this reason, it's always helpful to review the list of the most relevant parties involved in the matter with the attorney to ask about any pre-existing relationship. This conversation may also be an opportunity to ask your prospective attorney for references. Some law firms are hesitant to provide references and many former clients may be reluctant to provide either a written or verbal reference. Most litigants want to move on with other aspects of their lives after a legal dispute—even if they prevailed in their matter (any reference provided by an attorney would be a client who won their case, for obvious reasons). Yet, references are a standard practice in virtually every aspect of business—in fact, law firms themselves rely highly on references, particularly firms where landing a job offer as an associate is highly competitive. It never hurts to ask for references—especially if the facts and law are favorable to your case.

During the interviewing process, the attorney is also interviewing the prospective client. While you're seeking to understand if this person is the best legal representation you can find to successfully resolve your legal complaint, the lawyer is seeking to understand the merits of your case, whether or not the case is winnable based on the available facts and relative to the elements of the potential or existing compliant, if the case is within or beyond the timeframe of all applicable statutes of limitations, and if you're a reliable and reasonable client who will be easy to work with and—most importantly—have the ability to pay your legal bills.

There's a variety of reasons why an attorney will refuse to accept your case and not all—or even most—of the reasons are related to the merits of your case. Your case may not align with the business model of the attorney or law firm or your case may include involvement of potential bad acts by a fellow attorney. Some firms have a policy against filing lawsuits against other attorneys to avoid opposing parties who may be best equipped to propose a winning argument. Some attorneys may not think you have a full understanding of the financial expense required to fully litigate your complaint, may not think you can afford to fund your case, or may simply not want to work with you from a personality perspective.

Assuming the conflict check clears and the attorney is interested in representing you, the next step is the execution of a retainer agreement and the reaching of an agreement of standard fees and the initial retainer fee. In most circumstances, attorneys are paid by the hour—as a result many law firms measure attorney production by billable hour—and, in order to begin their representation of a client, a law firm will require an initial lump-sum retainer fee. This initial fee is paid upon the execution of the retainer agreement, the money is placed in a trust account, and the attorney bills against the existing money that the client has essentially pre-paid. Once the fee associated with billable hours exceeds the total agreed upon as the initial fee, the law firm will either bill monthly based on the agreed-upon hourly rate (generally referenced in the initial retainer agreement) or may request the client submit an additional retainer fee as prepayment for future billable hours.

> *There's a variety of reasons why an attorney will refuse to accept your case and not all—or even most— of the reasons are related to the merits of your case."*

The financial aspects of the legal representation are included in the retainer agreement as well as the scope of the legal work that is the basis of the agreement. For example, a defendant may hire a law firm as representation in response to a legal complaint that was already filed against the defendant. The retainer agreement may specify the law firm's representation as limited to the defendant's interest in the complaint already filed with the court. If a second plaintiff files a separate complaint against the defendant—regarding the same dispute or a completely unrelated controversy—the limited scope of the retainer agreement allows the law firm to decide whether or not they want to represent the defendant in the second lawsuit.

Understanding the process by which law firms will utilize the scope as defined within the retainer agreement to their advantage to maximize their flexibility with new clients is critical. A new client's ability to negotiate in terms of the scope of the representation is at its highest directly prior to signing the retainer agreement. Savvy clients will use this leverage to define the scope of the agreement to set specific goals with regard to the actions required by attorneys. If the facts of the case point to serving discovery requests to specific third parties or taking depositions from witnesses to the circumstances, it can be helpful to include these details within the retainer agreement to ensure the contract serves as an agreed-upon guide for the required legal work and approach to the case.

The final matter to inquire about during the hiring process is legal malpractice insurance. Lawyers purchase legal malpractice insurance to protect the firm from civil lawsuits that may be filed as a result of their legal work. Laws and regulations regarding legal malpractice insurance vary by state. Not every state requires lawyers to purchase insurance and not every state requires mandatory disclosure of whether or not the law firm is insured. Protexure Lawyers—an insurance company specializing in offering legal malpractice policies—offers a helpful overview of the related requirements placed upon lawyers on a state-by-state basis here[1]. In reviewing the state-specific requirements for legal malpractice insurance, some states require attorneys purchase coverage but the minimum coverage amount is not specified. There's a logical reason for this. Certain areas of the law—such as trust and estate law, personal injury, and legal transactions involving securities—may be at higher risk of a legal malpractice lawsuit and potential damages will vary widely both between different areas of the law and the circumstances of specific legal malpractice disputes. Yet, obtaining details regarding a potential law firm's malpractice coverage—whether they are insured and the total available policy—are much easier to obtain immediately prior to signing the retainer agreement—particularly when compared to a future time when there may be a true legal controversy regarding the lawyer's actions related to your case. The vast majority of

---

[1] https://blog.protexurelawyers.com/legal-malpractice-state-requirements

litigants won't ever need this information—and most people won't even need to ask about this topic—but, if your case is particularly high stakes with a potentially large award of damages, proactively requesting information regarding legal malpractice insurance may save time and hassle in the long term if your lawyer makes an unfortunate mistake or oversight.

Legal Payment Structures

Contingency or Hourly Fee

"An investment in knowledge pays the best interest."

— BENJAMIN FRANKLIN

This section is also not directly written for the benefit of self-represented litigants. Yet, it's included in this text for the benefit of a litigant who initially determined self-representation was the best strategy but eventually changed course and decided to hire an attorney. Additionally, this information could be helpful to self-represented clients in a case with an opposing party who is represented by a lawyer. It's likely difficult to determine the payment structure agreed upon between the opposing party and the opposing party's attorney—this is confidential information in most cases protected by attorney-client privilege that does not need to be disclosed. If you can infer the payment arrangement—potentially based on the opposing lawyer's behavior or the behavior of the opposing party—this may inform your own strategy and actions regarding the case.

When considering options for funding a legal fight, the most common arrangement between an attorney and client is an hourly fee structure. This approach, in the vast majority of cases, strongly favors the attorney. The client, particularly a client without much exposure to the practice of civil law, will likely have an exceedingly difficult time estimating the potential cost of a legal effort especially when the issue of controversy is complex and requires extensive litigation. The payment structure—agreed upon as a component within the initial retainer agreement signed at the onset of the relationship—will disclose the hourly rate for any lawyers (including partners and associates who often bill at different hourly rates), paralegals, and other support staff who may be involved in litigating the matter. The one component that will not be included is the estimated total hours of work required. As a result, the total billable hours—and the total legal bill for the endeavor—is not agreed upon at the inception of the relationship—which may lead to higher than estimated legal bills, an inability for the client to pay when the bills exceed the client's financial resources or willingness to spend additional funds on the effort, and unhappy attorney/client relationships. An exception to this guidance is simple matters of legal controversy such as a small claims complaint in which the damages, facts, and witnesses are all known and easily understood at the outset of the litigation. In a situation such as this, the potential damages are well understood and the simplicity of the case makes it easier for a client to assess the cost-effectiveness of pursuing the matter in civil court.

Given the fact that most lawyers build their business through referrals, client satisfaction gives an important incentive to provide fair value at an hourly rate and seek a positive resolution for your clients in a cost-effective manner. Yet, there are certainly attorneys with less-than-ethical business practices who may view the hourly rate fee structure as an opportunity to encourage clients to fight legal battles—and pay for them—when the facts and law don't necessarily justify the expense or—equally egregious—inflate billable hours with legal work that may or may not be required. Ethics codes in all state bar associations provide extensive guidance regarding an attorney's obligation to not adopt such unethical business practices as well as guidance for firms to govern the behavior of their organization.

Most clients will question their monthly statements and, especially if a client has limited experience in civil litigation, wonder about or even question the activities performed on their behalf as well as the associated cost. The vast majority of law firms and attorneys abide by the ethical guidelines set forth by their state bar association and adopt fair business practices that adhere to this guidance. Unfortunately, with an hourly fee structure, a new client needs to adopt a certain level of risk with regard to unethical billing practices when hiring an attorney—especially when considering the characteristics of the legal market that make it difficult to properly screen legal talent during the hiring process. The best practice for addressing this unavoidable situation is to ensure frequent and transparent communication regarding the legal activities the lawyer or team is pursuing, the purpose of each activity, the association between the activity and the end goal of resolving the case and—when required—a review of the monthly statements to ensure the activities and billable hours are properly reflected. It's important to remember a mistake can be misperceived as an intentional act of deceit with regard to billing without the benefit of open and honest discussion and a relationship built on trust. Most attorneys will be happy to discuss the details of their monthly statements as a means of ensuring client satisfaction and eliminating any potential misunderstanding that may be detrimental to the professional relationship.

Alternatively, some law firms—particularly in areas of the law which require extensive and expensive litigation—will consider agreeing to a contingency fee payment structure. With this arrangement, the lawyer agrees to represent the client in the matter at hand while deferring payment until the case is resolved. Contingency fee arrangements state that the attorney's compensation is "contingent upon" successfully resolving your case in a manner that results in either a settlement agreement or court judgment. If the client doesn't win, the attorney doesn't get paid.

The compensation is generally cited as a percentage of the award—either via settlement or judgment—with the percentage a negotiable figure. If a case is particularly complex, this would result in additional risk for the attorney and a higher percentage contingency fee. In many cases, the standard contingency fee is approximately 33 percent but, as a prospective client with a case that attorneys may consider assuming on a contingency basis, the percentage fee can be negotiated. The client's leverage is primarily associated with the strength of the case—as it pertains to known facts and circumstances relative to established case law. A stronger case would result in less risk to the law firm and, as a result, provide the prospective client with an argument to negotiate for a smaller percentage contingency fee.

Of course, the case still needs to be won! A prospective client is well-advised to recruit the strongest team of legal talent available in order to ensure a victory, even if this results in agreeing to a higher percentage with regard to a contingency fee. Additionally, the law in certain jurisdictions governs the use of contingency fees and may alleviate the need and/or ability to negotiate such arrangements. For example, some jurisdictions require contingency fees to be "reasonable"—which is one reason the 33 percent agreement has been widely adopted—while other jurisdictions govern contingency fees based on the total amount of damages awarded, grant the judge the ability to approve larger fees based on the particulars of the case, or specifically regulate the use of contingency fee arrangements in certain practices of the law (such as medical malpractice lawsuits).

By agreeing to a contingency fee arrangement, the most prevalent disadvantage a prospective client needs to consider is the fact that a successful resolution of your case may result in the law firm that represented you receiving higher compensation via a contingency fee arrangement than they would have received as a result of an hourly fee agreement. The fact that a contingency fee arrangement does not require any upfront capital certainly makes this an attractive option—particularly for clients who may not have cash reserves available to fund an extensive legal battle. If a client considers the business case associated with their legal endeavor—and you should—funding a legal battle via hourly fee arrangement may be justified if you can afford the expense and the strength of your case indicates a favorable outcome. Weighing the pros and cons of agreeing to a contingency arrangement—capital upfront, opportunity costs of that capital, and potential award upon completion—is a personal decision each client needs to consider with respect to their current financial position.

Another factor with regard to contingency fee arrangements is whether or not an attorney, or—more aptly—the attorney you think is best positioned to most-effectively represent you—is willing to agree to such a payment schedule. If an attorney is unwilling to agree to a contingency fee arrangement and insists upon an hourly fee structure, it's important to remember that this is simply a reflection of the attorney's opinion of your case within the parameters of this one attorney's specific framework of risk. A single attorney's insistence upon an hourly fee arrangement is not necessarily a conclusion regarding the strength of your case or the lawyer's confidence in your argument prevailing in court. Many attorneys simply refuse to consider contingency fee arrangements as a policy for the firm as a result of any number of factors including the strength of their existing caseload—and, on a related note, their existing revenue stream—or an aversion to the risk associated with representing clients on a contingency fee basis due to past experience or the fact that this would conflict with their business model. Certain legal specialties—personal injury and employment law including workplace discrimination and sexual harassment complaints—are more likely to enter contingency fee agreements compared to other areas of the law. If your case is in an area of the law which doesn't typically offer contingency fee arrangements, it's unlikely you'll find an attorney who will make an exception for you except in the most extraordinary circumstances.

One final, and important, disadvantage to contingency fee arrangements that needs to be considered is the tax implications of successfully receiving a settlement or judgment in your favor when represented by an attorney via contingency fee agreement. As a result of the 2017 Tax Cut and Jobs Act, attorneys' fees are no longer tax deductible which may result in a legal party being liable—from a tax perspective—for the entirety of a monetary legal award including the portion of the award that was earned by their lawyers and paid at settlement per the contingency fee agreement. In other words, the entirety of the money secured in a successful lawsuit may become taxable income for the prevailing party—including the portion of the money the lawyer receives.

There are exceptions to this "contingency fee tax trap"—for instance, funds secured in cases that involve physical injury or plaintiffs' cases where legal fees can be considered a business expense—are exempt from this tax implication. This complicated area of the law requires guidance from an expert who can consider all the particulars of your case (a good overview of the issues can be found here[1]). Tax implications are an important factor in assessing your options regarding the funding of a legal endeavor—particularly if the potential financial stakes are high.

In addition to hourly fee and contingency fee arrangements, there are other alternatives available for the funding of legal efforts. Contingency-hourly and mixed hourly-contingency arrangements may also be worth discussing with potential lawyers and law firms during the hiring process. In a contingency-hourly payment arrangement, payment is delayed until the case results in a financial award (either via judgment or set-

---

[1] https://news.bloombergtax.com/daily-tax-report/insight-the-contingency-fee-tax-trap-and-a-solution

tlement). Payment of the legal bill is delayed but governed by billable hours and the agreed-upon hourly rate.

> *Many attorneys simply refuse to consider contingency fee arrangements as a policy for the firm as a result of any number of factors including the strength of their existing caseload—and, on a related note, their existing revenue stream—or an aversion to the risk associated with representing clients on a contingency fee basis due to past experience or the fact that this would conflict with their business model."*

In mixed hourly-contingency payment arrangements (also known as hybrid payment arrangements), the attorney agrees to represent a client with a lower-than-standard hourly rate and a percentage on contingency as potential long-term inducement in the event the case is successfully resolved. This type of arrangement benefits both parties from a cash-flow perspective. The client is paying for legal representation at a discount while the lawyer is maintaining a certain level of minimum cash flow to fund activities with the potential for a larger payout in the future. This also reduces the risk for the law firm, compared to a standard contingency fee arrangement, by ensuring some level of income attached to the matter in the event the case is not resolved successfully, the client decides to change their legal representation, or a non-cash–based settlement is reached (which is more likely in commercial litigation). For additional context related to this innovative fee structure, this article[2] is particularly informative.

Each of the outlined payment structures is worth exploring during the hiring process. This type of exploratory conver-

---

[2] https://www.plaintiffmagazine.com/recent-issues/item/hybrid-fee-agreements-for-business-litigation

sation will also demonstrate to your attorney a willingness on your behalf to act as a consulting partner in this legal matter as well as provide an opportunity to assess your ability to collaborate with the prospective attorney(s) you're considering hiring before signing a retainer agreement. If your attorney approaches this conversation in the spirit of partnership, this is a good indication of your ability to successfully work together during the litigation process. If not, this may become a factor to consider as you continue to interview attorneys and conduct your due diligence during the hiring process.

Evaluating the Strength of Your Case

The Business Decision of Filing a Civil Lawsuit

"The less I understood of this farrago, the less I was in a position to understand its importance."

— ROBERT LOUIS STEVENSON, *DR JEKYLL AND MR HYDE*

After filing a complaint or being informed a complaint was filed, the litigant's singular focus needs to be the ongoing evaluation of the strength of the case *as it currently stands,* combined with a continual appraisal of potential new evidence that may strengthen or weaken the case. In parallel, the other guiding principle for successfully navigating the civil legal system is the monitoring of the current and anticipated cost burden of your civil suit relative to the potential damages associated with your case.

Participation in the civil justice system is, at heart, a business decision. With some exceptions, money is the primary method of rewarding a successful argument from the perspective of both the plaintiff and defendant. As a result, the business case comparing cost with potential financial award needs to be at the center of the litigant's decision with regard to initial and continual participation. It's difficult to ignore the emotional impact of any situation that leads to litigation. It's tempting to use the civil justice system to express an opinion, ensure your voice is heard, pursue revenge or—for a variety of reasons as diverse as the human condition—seek resolution and closure to a difficult and charged situation. If the goal of any civil litigation isn't the pursuit of financial damages—either as an award for plaintiffs or attorneys' fees and a potential countersuit as a defendant—it's likely time to reevaluate your plan to pursue justice in the civil courts. Depending on the evidence already secured, contacting law enforcement in an attempt to raise concerns regarding potential criminal actions may be a better path toward resolution. The pursuit of both criminal justice and civil justice—not uncommon—may also be worth investigating. Yet, it's important to understand that the primary means of resolution within the civil justice system is financial in nature. Many first-time litigants—depending on the situation—may consider a financial payout at the end of civil litigation as somehow compromising. A financial award may be viewed as insufficient when considering the egregious acts and behavior that lead them to a courtroom in the first place. Of course, that perspective may change once the check clears but—if it doesn't—the litigant needs to enter the legal arena understanding that monetary award—insufficient as it may be in some circumstances—is most likely the only recourse available; at least within the civil justice system.

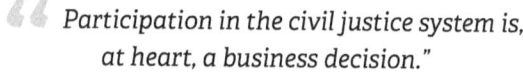 *Participation in the civil justice system is, at heart, a business decision."*

Once you've come to terms with the fact that your civil lawsuit is simply a business decision—regardless of the circumstances that preceded the filing of the complaint—and you've defined financial parameters that guide your actions—the next step is to determine the strength of your case today and identify potential paths of discovery that may either strengthen or weaken your overall argument. The most logical method of evaluating your case—the approach used by diligent and responsible attorneys—is to align the facts with the law. If you're a plaintiff, identify the potential statute or statutes that may apply and compare the facts as they're known today with the set of elements associated with each relevant statute. In the civil law code, each statute includes a description of the elements of the statute. Legal elements are essentially the set of facts, aligned with the law, required for a plaintiff to prove their case.

For example, if a plaintiff references "breach of contract" as the cause of their legal action the plaintiff will need to prove to following to prevail with their lawsuit:

1. A contract exists between the two relevant parties.
    a. The defendant was aware of and entered into the contract.
2. The defendant intentionally took an action, or actions, to knowingly breach the existing contract (in other words, there is no legal justification for the defendant's actions).
3. The actions of the defendant resulted in quantifiable monetary damages to the plaintiff (in other words, there's a path toward resolution for the court in the form of a monetary award).

In many cases, there may be multiple statutes that may apply to a specific legal issue. For example, a plaintiff may have the justification to file a complaint based on a variety of statutes in response to the same bad acts related to theft of their inheritance including tortious interference of inheritance, tortious interference of contract, breach of fiduciary duty, or financial exploitation of the elderly. Please note that the elements associated with different statutes—even the existence of different statutes—can differ from state-to-state and between state and federal courts.

Each of the preceding statutes features different elements required for the plaintiff to meet their legal burden. As a plaintiff, deciding which statute to reference in your initial complaint with regard to the known facts *at the time* of the complaint is critical to focusing your efforts. After all, discovery is essentially the pursuit of facts that allow you to meet the other elements of the statute not yet proven. If you're the defendant in a civil complaint, assessing the known facts of the situation as these facts relate to the elements of the statute referenced in the complaint, or any other applicable statutes, is fundamental in determining your potential liability.

In the event a complaint is filed in which the plaintiff is initially able to meet some—but not all—of the elements of the statute, the bulk of the legal effort will be related to finding evidence that allows you to meet the currently unmet elements of the statute. In the breach of contract example cited previously, it may be indisputable that a contract exists between the two parties. For instance, a contract is entered into evidence that was signed by both parties and the defendant doesn't dispute the validity of the contract. Element number one of the statute is now met and the focus remains on the remaining elements. The defendant and the plaintiff may not agree on the whether or not potentially bad acts constitute a breach of contract—the terms of the contract and potential provisions that may justify or restrict such actions—whether or not the potential bad act occurred at all or—if the parties agree that the act occurred— whether or not the bad act inflicted monetary damage upon the plaintiff. Contracts can be complicated and legal contractual disputes—often heavily reliant upon differing interpretations of contracts—can make a situation that is already confusing increasingly confounding.

If the facts are on your side, argue the facts. If the law is on your side, argue the law. Arguing the facts means, or should mean, obtaining the most relevant facts to ensure you're able to meet every element within the statute. It's much easier to argue the facts if you have all the facts. In the breach of contract example above, the plaintiff may claim a contract with the real estate developer building their new home included a provision specifying the use of high-quality fixtures in the kitchen and bathrooms prior to taking possession of the home. The contract may also include a provision that states this work needs to be completed in order to meet the terms of the contract and complete the defined scope of work. In order to prove the fact that the real estate developer breached their contract by failing to install high-quality fixtures in the kitchen and bathrooms, the plaintiff may need to obtain current photos of the house that detail either a lack of installed fixtures or installed fixtures that don't meet the quality level as specified in the contract.

> ❝ *If the facts are on your side, argue the facts. If the law is on your side, argue the law."*

If you're the plaintiff, you need to ask yourself how difficult—and expensive—it may be to obtain the photos required to support your breach of contract argument. If the real estate developer still has possession of the house, they may present any number of hurdles—both within the realm of the courts and outside of the legal arena—to prevent you from obtaining the photos. If a third party has taken possession of the house—for instance, a bank—that may make it a little easier for the plaintiff to obtain the required photos. After all, the fact that the bank isn't the opposing party in this example leads us to the logical conclusion that the bank may be more forthcoming with information that may help the plaintiff's case. But the plaintiff can't assume the bank—as a third party—will automatically act as a neutral party. The bank may have a long-established relationship with the real estate developer that they don't want to jeopardize or the bank may be aware of another breach of contract—a breach that may be the bank's fault and may even introduce liability to the bank with regard to this fraught situation—which may provide a disincentive for the bank to fully cooperate.

In this example, I'm not suggesting either the real estate developer or the bank will not follow the Rules of Civil Procedure—though there are certainly plenty of bad actors who do everything in their power to avoid compliance with the rules of the civil code if compliance is a risk to them. The opposing party or the third party may simply make it more difficult for the plaintiff. This may result in delayed responses to discovery requests which may require the filing of a motion to compel to ensure compliance (a filing that will increase both the legal fees of the plaintiff and the time required to litigate the issue) or incomplete responses that comply with the exact wording of the request but may not include all relevant information.

With this in mind, a savvy plaintiff will attempt to determine the likelihood of cooperation in response to a discovery request—either from the opposing party or a third party—as well as evaluate the potential cost associated with the discovery effort in terms of both time and financial expense. Given the complexities of the legal system, it's incredibly difficult to establish precise figures but this type of analysis is invaluable both as a means of directing your legal efforts and a method to continually scrutinize the business case associated with the legal endeavor.

The Importance of Legal Venue and Jurisdiction

"Good lawyers know the law. Great lawyers know the judge."

— ANONYMOUS

When a plaintiff files a legal complaint, an oft-overlooked component of the strategy is the choice of venue and court of jurisdiction that will be most sympathetic to the plaintiff's argument based on both the local legal statutes and the relevant facts of the case. Venue is simply the physical location of the court that will hear the case and jurisdiction is the authority of that court to hear arguments and, ultimately, impose a judgment. When considering the fact that the legal system is built upon the *interpretation* of the law, a sophisticated legal team will understand how the existing case law may impact the interpretation of the various facts and circumstances of your case as it relates to the trial courts in the different districts within the state. As a result, a plaintiff may determine it's best to file a complaint within a specific county that may be more favorable than the trial court in a different county. Conversely, a defendant—upon being served the complaint—may decide to file a motion requesting a change of venue to a court that the defendant perceives will be more favorable to their argument. As a self-represented litigant, it may be difficult to determine the venue likely to be most favorable to your argument. Yet, time spent networking with individuals—

attorneys, fellow litigants, court workers and administrators—to ask for insight prior to filing may allow you to gain a basic level of understanding about a specific court's biases with regard to the subject of your lawsuit.

This practice is sometimes referred to dismissively as "court-shopping"—particularly in legal arguments that relate to venue. This concept may have a negative connotation but, in reality, court-shopping is a good description for the pursuit of a favorable venue. In addition, the rules of procedure that govern civil law also restrict a litigant's ability to pursue justice only to the courts that have jurisdiction over the matter of controversy. The party needs to meet the local court's requirements—either by virtue of residence or the fact that the bad act allegedly occurred in the court's district. Of course, legal parties can be quite creative in developing arguments to justify the relevance of a matter to a legal venue but the Rules of Civil Procedure are designed to limit egregious court-shopping.

Venue and jurisdiction are two separate, but related, legal concepts. Jurisdiction is the principle that a court of law has the authority to determine legal claims. Venue is the physical location of the court where the lawsuit will be filed and the case will be heard. A venue, or court, needs to have jurisdiction in order for the court's decision to hold legal merit and be enforceable. There are two primary matters of jurisdiction to be considered—personal jurisdiction and subject matter jurisdiction. Personal jurisdiction is, in most cases, fairly straightforward. For example, a state court has jurisdiction over someone who's a resident of the state or a business that operates in the state. As is typical of every legal concept, exceptions exist and laws are written to either include or exclude such exceptions. A person only briefly visiting a state can, generally, be sued in the state court if the facts and circumstances of the lawsuit are related to a time period when a state's non-resident was in the state. On a related note, if a business does not have a physical presence in a given state but it can be reasonably argued conducts business in the state—for instance, offering a product online and shipping the product to the state's residents—the relevant state's court system will likely have jurisdiction over the business. From a practical standpoint, a lawsuit generally needs to be filed in the county in which at least one of the litigants resides or the county where the events related to the legal controversy took place.

> " Venue and jurisdiction are two separate, but related, legal concepts. Jurisdiction is the principle that a court of law has the authority to determine legal claims. Venue is the physical location of the court where the lawsuit will be filed and the case will be heard."

Subject matter jurisdiction can be more complex as compared to personal jurisdiction but, in some cases, is well worth the effort to understand the potential benefits specific choices may have with regard to your case. Subject matter jurisdiction relates to the choice between federal and state courts. In order for a lawsuit to be heard by a federal court, the case needs to involve a federal question of the law or involve legal parties with diversity of citizenship—meaning litigants from two or more different states. Additionally, a lawsuit filed in federal court as a result of a diversity of citizenship also needs to include potential damages of more than $75,000.

When a case is filed in federal court referencing a federal question, the guiding document for deciding the outcome of the case in the United States Constitution and when a federal case is filed via the diversity of citizenship the statutes codified within federal law are the basis of the case. Examples of the types of controversies that may justify a federal lawsuit related to Constitutional matters and rights outlined in the Constitution such as the freedom of speech, freedom of assembly, freedom of the press or freedom of religion. Federal cases related to Constitutional law generally involve significant legal matters that have the potential to profoundly impact our society.

With regard to federal cases related to diversity of citizenship, as long as the potential damages exceed $75,000 the case is eligible to be heard in federal court and—as a result—be subject to federal law. If the case meets these two requirements, the federal case does not need to have a federal question as the matter of controversy.

While the vast majority of civil cases in the United States are heard within the various state's trial courts rather than the federal court system, there are certainly situations in which the federal court may be more sympathetic to your argument. The best way to determine the most favorable venue and jurisdiction is by returning to the basic examination of the facts and circumstances of your case as it relates to case law. When comparing the risks and benefits of a state trial court with the federal court, examine the facts and circumstances with regard to the elements of the law for both the relevant state statutes and potentially applicable federal statutes. It's also important to remember that a lawsuit can be initially filed within a state court and remove the case—the legal phrase for transfer—to federal court if the case fulfills the diversity of jurisdiction requirements.

The Phases of a Lawsuit

*"You get justice in the next world,
in this world you have the law."*

— WILLIAM GADDIS, *A FROLIC OF HIS OWN*

The many, varied facets of the law ensure that there's no such thing as a guaranteed outcome in a legal setting. Yet, the Rules of Civil Procedure are designed to provide a process—it's also helpful to think of it as a framework—to ensure a consistent method for the resolution of civil complaints. No case is the same—even cases with the exact same set of facts and circumstances may resolve in different manners—but the rules governing the process are designed to inject some degree of certainty into an inherently uncertain process. Of course, if there's anything that can be considered universal in the law is that rules, not to mention facts, are subject to interpretation. With all this ambiguity, understanding the various phases of a lawsuit that are ubiquitous within the law is helpful when considering the effort required to prevail in a court of law. This section, and the sections that follow, are intended to provide the reader with a practical and accessible framework for the "typical" lawsuit within the civil courts.

In the previous section, the difference between a grievance and an actionable legal complaint was outlined as well as the best practice for evaluating the viability of a legal complaint by comparing the facts and circumstances of the situation with the elements required to win in a court of law. The filing of a legal complaint in a relevant court of law—ideally referencing the relevant civil statute or statutes most applicable to the case—is the first step required to initiate legal proceedings. Once this step is taken, the following represents a general overview of the process adhered to within the civil courts—with the important caveat that every lawsuit is unique, lawsuits don't always advance in a linear fashion, and determining a timeline toward resolution is often difficult. This is particularly true when a lawsuit involves a complicated set of facts and/or legal principles and the applicable case law is subject to interpretation and legal disputes related to this interpretation (which, in theory, is every case though—in practice—the damages available in some cases don't justify such extensive legal wrangling).

1. *Phase One:* Developing a complaint and filing a lawsuit with a civil court that has jurisdiction to resolve the legal controversy

2. *Phase Two:* The discovery process used by both the plaintiff and defendant to gather evidence that supports the case of each litigant

3. *Phase Three:* Mediation—either initiated voluntarily or required by law or judicial decree—as a method of resolving the legal complaint via settlement agreement without the court making a determination

4. *Phase Four:* A trial which allows each litigant to present their case, comprised of both supportive facts and case law, to a judge and/or jury of their peers

5. *Phase Five:* The appeal process which allows a litigant to ask a higher court to overrule the lower court's decision either with respect to the verdict or a ruling made by the judge within the course of the case

6. *Phase Six:* Post-judgment activities—most often the collection of damages or the imposition of one of the litigant's rights, but this phase may also include other post-trial activities such as a criminal referral to law enforcement authorities based on the facts and circumstances of the case as well as the case's outcome

The framework above is simply a guideline for the manner in which the standard lawsuit (which, again, doesn't exist) is supposed to unfold. Exceptions abound. For example, a judge may grant a defendant's motion to dismiss and force the plaintiff to file a new complaint—essentially reverting to phase one—based on the facts of the case as they relate to the elements of a specific statute. Or a judge's procedural decision, for instance whether or not evidence is admissible, may result in one of the litigants filing an appeal to a higher court in an attempt to overturn the judge's ruling—which would prevent the lawsuit from proceeding to the next phase until the issue is resolved. There are countless examples of specific circumstances that may impact the course of a legal proceeding, and prevent a lawsuit from advancing in a linear fashion, but the framework above provides an overview of the general process within civil law. One more caveat prior to continuing the overview, many lawsuits—the data shows the vast majority—don't ever proceed to trial. For example, legal disputes can be dropped by the plaintiff or a settlement agreement between litigants may be reached at any time during the process—including during the course of the trial—which is often referred to as a "courtroom steps" settlement agreement.

> " *The framework above is simply a guideline for the manner in which the standard lawsuit (which, again, doesn't exist) is supposed to unfold.* "

Phase One:
The Initiation of a
Lawsuit

"Silence is sometimes an argument of consent."

— THOMAS HOBBES

The first step required to initiate a legal dispute is the filing of a complaint with a cause of action by the plaintiff. The complaint is an official legal document that details the facts and circumstances of the disagreement including a justification for filing the lawsuit—referred to as a cause of action. This justification describes how the defendant's actions violated the rights of the plaintiff and includes specifics that correlate the facts and circumstances of the controversy with the elements of the civil statute cited. The cause of action within the complaint is intended to provide proof that the actions of the defendant justify the plaintiff's complaint as a means of obtaining remuneration, property, or the enforcement of a legal right.

> *The complaint is an official legal document that details the facts and circumstances of the disagreement including a justification for filing the lawsuit—referred to as a cause of action."*

Developing a solid argument to convince the judge of the validity of the complaint and cause of action is crucial given the fact that the defendant will also have the opportunity to answer the complaint in a similarly binding legal document—often referred to as an "Answer and Defense." In the defendant's answer, the defendant is granted the analogous opportunity to present their case. Additionally, the defendant also has the opportunity—after the initial filing of the complaint or at any time during the process—to file a motion to dismiss which would effectively end the lawsuit. Given the authority of the judge to determine whether or not a complaint is valid in the eyes of the law and the opportunities afforded to the defendant to, potentially, effectively prevent a full hearing of the facts, it's imperative that the plaintiff develop an indisputable and compelling cause of action to ensure the lawsuit proceeds.

Assuming the judge agrees with the plaintiff's cause of action and views the facts and circumstances as sufficient to justify a lawsuit, the lawsuit begins to advance through the various steps as outlined within the Rules of Civil Procedure.

The Motion to Dismiss

"He who establishes his argument by noise and command shows that his reason is weak."

— MICHEL DE MONTAIGNE

A consideration of the motion to dismiss is perfectly situated immediately after a description of the process for initiating a lawsuit given the fact that a motion to dismiss is often the first step the defense will take in response to the initial filing of a complaint. The motion will include a legal justification for the judge to dismiss the case based on the facts, circumstances and applicable case law related to the complaint. A motion to dismiss is a definitive and final decision that effectively stops the lawsuit from proceeding beyond its current stage. When a motion to dismiss is granted, all activity is ceased and the lawsuit is over—a daunting possibility for a plaintiff who just went through the process of hiring an attorney and filing a legal complaint. The granting of motion to dismiss can be heartbreaking to a plaintiff who thinks a bad act has occurred and considers the court system as the only path toward resolution.

The legal reasoning detailed within a motion to dismiss is, of course, customized based on the particulars of a specific complaint but a few of the common reasons cited within such a motion include the following:

- *A failure to state a claim* which posits that, even if all the facts detailed by the plaintiff are true, the facts don't justify a cause of action—effectively, the defendant is claiming they're actions do not justify a legal proceeding even if all facts are taken as evidence.

  This possible argument reinforces the importance of the exercise to choose the statute that best aligns with the facts of the case and communicate, within the initial complaint, how the facts of the case will enable the plaintiff to meet each of the elements of the statute.

- *The court does not have jurisdiction over either the litigants*—also known as personal jurisdiction—or the subject matter (for example, a lawsuit filed in federal court that does not involve parties with a diversity of citizenship or potential damages that exceed $75,000).

  Developing the specifics to justify the fact that the court in which the complaint was filed has both personal and subject matter jurisdiction prior to filing the initial complaint can allow a plaintiff to proactively deflect this argument.

- *Inadequate, incomplete, or unsatisfactory service of process.* In other words, the plaintiff did not follow the Rules of Civil Procedure by failing to serve the defendant with notice of the complaint including the court summons and a copy of the complaint (referred to as service of process).

Employing a reputable process server who understands the rules and creates an indisputable paper trail is the best way to avoid this potential argument.

- **The venue is improper** based on the litigants involved in the dispute and/or the jurisdiction of the court (both personal and subject matter jurisdiction)—in other words, the court is the wrong court in which to hold this legal proceeding.

  A common resolution to this argument is to transfer the case to a different venue—rather than an outright dismissal of the case. Yet, you may think one venue may provide a strategic advantage due to the relevant statutes that apply, the potential for judges to be sympathetic to your argument or, even –personal relationships your legal team may have with the judges in a certain venue that may provide insight into the types of arguments that may be persuasive. If this is an important strategic decision, one approach may be to identify other cases—similar to your own—which were heard by your team's preferred venue.

- **The statute of limitations has expired** and, as a result, the plaintiff no longer has the legal grounds, or right, to sue the defendant.

  The statute of limitations is the time period in which a plaintiff has the right to file a complaint based on when the cause of action occurred. Filing a motion to dismiss based on the statute of limitations is a method often deployed by defense attorneys that can be effective—remember, it provides an already overwhelmed court with a legally justifiable excuse to dismiss a complaint. It's important to remember—particularly as a plaintiff—that the statute of limitations has many variables including the time when the statute begins to toll—in other words, the time when the clock for the statute of limitations begins to tick. For example, if a breach of contract factually occurred ten years ago and the statute of limitations is four years, a plaintiff who only discovered the breach three months ago (potentially due to the fact that the defendant failed to disclose evidence that would have divulged the breach) would still have standing to proceed and the statute of limitations would not apply as a valid legal justification for dismissal.

If the defendant can successfully argue that the lawsuit should be dismissed based on one of the above legal arguments, the defendant is able to avoid the expense, in both time and money, associated with a lawsuit and avert any potential damages. Given the serious implications of granting a motion to dismiss, the legal argument needs to be informed by the relevant facts of the case as well as the associated case law. Judges, in most cases, want to preserve a litigant's right to their day in court—which makes the burden for granting a motion to dismiss fairly high. Yet, the volume of cases on each court's docket and the fact that most civil courts are overwhelmed with the sheer volume of complaints creates an incentive that encourages the dismissal of cases if it can be reasonably argued that the case was filed without merit.

The above describes the process of obtaining an involuntary dismissal, by court order, of a lawsuit. This is the most common situation when a legal professional describes the risks or rewards associated with a motion to dismiss—depending on whether the party is the plaintiff or the defendant. At any time, a defendant can file a motion to dismiss which can effectively end the lawsuit. As a result, it's important to keep the potential justifications for a motion to dismiss in mind as new evidence is discovered.

> **“** Judges, in most cases, want to preserve a litigant's
> right to their day in court—which makes the burden
> for granting a motion to dismiss fairly high. ”

There also exists the option for a plaintiff to file a voluntary motion to dismiss—effectively dropping their lawsuit—that can be issued with or without a court order. A plaintiff may determine that the discovery of new facts will prevent the successful resolution of the case, the time and expense associated with the legal dispute outweighs the potential reward or that there's an alternative method for resolving the legal dispute. The most prevalent alternative method of resolution is a settlement agreement reached by the litigants without the intervention of the court. When this occurs, the lawyer(s) or self-represented litigants will also ask the court to issue a motion to dismiss to finalize the matter—and submit a copy of the signed settlement agreement as an exhibit with the motion to dismiss.

The Motion for Summary Judgment

"Everything has to come to an end, sometime."

— L. FRANK BAUM, *THE MARVELOUS LAND OF OZ*

A motion for summary judgment may have a more innocuous name than a motion to dismiss but, if the judge rules against you in a hearing on this motion, the impact can be just as profound. The particulars differ when considering a motion for dismissal and a motion for summary judgment but the result, if successful, can be the same—the end of your day in court. The filing of a motion for summary judgment will usually get the attention of the non-movant's legal team due to the serious implications associated with the motion—if the motion is granted the complaint is dismissed and all proceedings cease.

By filing a motion for summary judgment, the movant—also known as the party filing the motion—is making an argument to the court that no reasonable factfinder, such as a judge and/or jury, could disagree with the conclusion as stated in the motion. The details will differ in terms of the legal reasoning but the request is always the same—that the factfinder should rule in the movant's favor and dismiss the case. The primary nuance with a motion for summary judgment is that the motion must unequivocally state that there is no disputed issue of material fact. In other words, the filing party is stating that they are entitled to judgment in their favor by law even if all facts are assumed as true and viewed in the most favorable light for the opposing party. A motion for summary judgment is inherently a fairly extreme measure. As such, the motion is only granted when the legal conclusion is ruled, by a judge, to be indisputable even when all facts are viewed from the perspective that most favors the non-movant party. The legal standard for granting a motion for summary judgment is fairly clear but the professional dynamics involved further decrease the likelihood that a judge will grant the motion. Given the fact that judges don't want to be overruled on appeal, the inherently technical nature of summary judgment arguments and the motion's reliance on the law—rather than the facts related to the controversy—summary judgment rulings are candidates for appeal. As a result, most judges are reluctant to grant such a motion. On the other hand, every judge's docket has a backlog of cases and a summary judgment decision is one way to address the overwhelming caseload.

A litigant can file a motion for summary judgment—which is requesting the complete dismissal of the case—or a partial motion for summary judgment—which is a request for clarity regarding an issue before the court. A partial motion for summary judgment is an effort by one party to establish as certain the court's legal opinion with regard to a component of the case. The motion for partial summary judgment is not requesting a dismissal of the case—the purpose is to ask for the court's ruling on one element of the case.

> " *The primary nuance with a motion for summary judgment is that the motion must unequivocally state that there is no disputed issue of material fact."*

The partial motion for summary judgment allows the litigants to strategically direct efforts based on the understanding derived from the ruling as opposed to the need to develop strategies and contingencies based on multiple potential rulings and/or understandings from the court. Similar to a motion for summary judgment, the movant party filing a partial motion for summary judgment is asking the court to issue a ruling of law with the caveat that all facts are undisputed and viewed from the perspective most favorable to the opposing party. Interestingly, both successful or unsuccessful motions for partial summary judgment will inform both parties' legal strategies as the case advances.

A great example of a common application for the partial motion for summary judgment is an effort to obtain a ruling from the court related to the statute of limitations. For example, the statute of limitations for a breach of fiduciary duty complaint in Florida is four years. Yet, the outcome of the entire case may rely on the date when the clock begins to toll on the case. In other words, what is the specific date when the statute of limitations begins? The most obvious timeframe for the clock to begin to toll is the date when the breach of the fiduciary duty occurred. Of course, as with most issues related to civil law, the statute of limitations can be extremely complicated. It may also be argued that the clock begins to toll—the statute of limitations begins—when the affected party discovers the bad act. In this interpretation of the statute of limitations, the clock may not begin to many years after the actual date of the bad act. In this example, a defendant may file a motion for summary judgment arguing that the statute of limitations has already expired and—regardless of any facts that may be presented by the plaintiff—the law states the case should be dismissed. Alternatively, the plaintiff may file a partial motion for summary judgment seeking a ruling from the court on when the statute of limitations begins to toll. If the court rules against the plaintiff and rules that the statute of limitations has already expired, the plaintiff may decide to drop their case. This certainty may save the plaintiff significant time and money. On the other hand, if the motion is decided in the plaintiff's favor and the judge rules that the statute of limitations begins when the bad act was discovered, this may give the plaintiff the understanding required to confidently proceed with the case.

Once a motion for summary judgment or partial summary judgment is filed, the next step is a hearing with the judge. The movant has filed the original motion, the non-movant—in most cases—has filed a response to the motion and, in an ideal world, the judge has read both filings.

The purpose of the summary judgment hearing is primarily to allow the judge to ask questions of the respective attorneys or self-represented litigants. A hearing related to a summary judgment motion has very specific rules by which it must be conducted. The hearing is not a trial—though lawyers often refer to it as a mini-trial. Witnesses are not called and the only evidence allowed is evidence already admitted into the court record as a result of previous legal proceedings within the case. The judge will often allow oral arguments which, depending on the judge, can be a good opportunity for the judge to question each attorney or self-represented litigant regarding their respective arguments as well as previously submitted filings and motions. It's also critical to appreciate the fact that the judge has no discretion regarding any fact related to the controversy. Previously, we stated that the motion for summary judgment requires an assumption of favorability for the non-movant party with regard to all available facts. This assumption applies to the judge, who is not allowed to interpret or express an opinion regarding the credibility of witnesses or the viability of facts presented as evidence. As a result, the motion for summary judgment inherently raises questions of the law—not factual questions. Examples include statute of limitations issues, a party's standing to bring the complaint, venue and jurisdiction controversies, and the principle of *res judicata* (an argument that states the legal matter has already been litigated by an appropriate court and may not be relitigated).

Given the fact that the facts within a summary judgment hearing are indisputable, one obvious path for overcoming a summary judgment motion is to prove that the facts are, actually, in dispute. Of course, the party filing the summary judgment motion needs to argue that the facts are, in fact, indisputable.

Defendants are more likely to file a motion for summary judgment—in most cases to establish a ruling in favor of its affirmative defense. In this case, the defendant is simply asking the court to assert that the defendant's defense is accurate and a trial is not required. Conversely, a defendant may file a motion for summary judgment asking the judge to rule that the plaintiff can't prove one of the essential elements within the plaintiff's complaint. If the judge rules in the defendant's favor by stating one of the elements of the plaintiff's complaint is invalid, the entire complaint is automatically dismissed. This tactic—essentially finding the single flaw in a plaintiff's complaint—is a common defense attorney tactic.

Plaintiffs less commonly file a motion for summary judgment, but the possibility exists. In this situation, the plaintiff is asking the court to rule in their favor regarding an element or elements of their cause of action. For example, if a plaintiff already has sufficient evidence to convince a judge to rule in their favor, the plaintiff may file a motion for summary judgment asking the court for a ruling and requesting the judge advance the case to a hearing about damages.

There are a number of risks inherent in filing a motion for summary judgment. Most significantly, given the high standard required for a favorable ruling the motion may not succeed and the movant party may spend significant time and money on a fruitless pursuit. Depending on the specifics of the case, a successful motion may require extensive discovery and/or the solicitation of expert witness testimony—all of which will increase your legal expenses. Of course, that may be the point. A well-funded litigant may file extensive motions—including a motion for summary judgment—in order to force the other side to spend money and effort combatting the motion(s). Finally, a motion for summary judgment will likely require that the filing party reveal their best arguments. If the motion is unsuccessful, the opposing party will have more time to prepare for a compelling counter-argument in advance of a potential trial.

There are also plenty of compelling reasons to file a motion for summary judgment. Most obviously, the defendant can get the case dismissed with one motion and a related hearing. Even if the motion is unsuccessful, the effort will likely force the opposing party to reveal their legal strategy, or at least a portion of their strategy. For example, a motion for summary judgment may force the other party to expose the identity of their expert witnesses or even the testimony expert witnesses are likely to provide at trial. This glimpse into the opposing party's strategy provides insight when preparing to cross-examine the expert witness or recruit your own expert witness to provide alternative testimony.

Another potential benefit of filing a motion for summary judgment is a narrowing of the issues to be considered within the case. The judge may not rule in favor of the entire motion but may narrow the other party's claims as a result of the motion for summary judgment. This allows the party who filed the motion to focus on elements of the complaint deemed valid by the court—which will be useful in directing strategic efforts, not to mention save time and legal expenses.

Finally, the non-filing party needs to be prepared to make a compelling argument against the motion for summary judgment. A motion for summary judgment may arrive on the opposing party's schedule at a time when they're unprepared or distracted. Defending against a motion for summary judgment is high stakes and requires a focused argument with a well-considered legal strategy. Filing a motion for summary judgment forces the other side to make an argument whether they're ready or not.

Phase Two:
The Legal Discovery
Process

*"Facts are stubborn things; and whatever may be our
wishes, our inclinations, or the dictates of passion, they
cannot alter the state of facts and evidence."*

— JOHN ADAMS, *THE PORTABLE JOHN ADAMS*

In most legal television shows and movies, the culmination of the narrative is the trial. In the world of fiction, the trial gives the story the dramatic arc and suspense that's a feature of the genre but in the real world most cases are won or lost during the discovery phase. This critical time period consists of motions and counter-filings, the exchange of documentation that may or may not be relevant, and depositions—sometimes lasting hours or even days—of the parties to the lawsuit as well as any number of third parties and experts. The goal of the plaintiff is the introduction of evidence that will enable them to meet the various elements of the complaint. The defendant wants to introduce evidence that may be exonerating while also preventing the introduction of evidence that may be damaging. Evidence—either favorable or unfavorable to either specific party—needs to not only be identified but also introduced via a court-sanctioned process. This process is defined broadly as discovery and consists of a variety of different avenues including the following:

- Interrogatories
- Requests for production
- Depositions
- Affidavits

In addition to the overarching goal of securing evidence, the discovery process can also serve to augment your overall legal strategy. Both sides have the ability to request information in the various forms as well as the obligation to comply with the other side's requests. One example of the discovery process as a tactic in the overall legal strategy is the fact that one party may leverage the process to impose a burden upon the other party. This burden can surface in a wide variety of forms. Most commonly, a discovery request imposes both a burden of time / effort upon the respondent as well as a financial burden. One of the most effective ways to increase the other parties' legal expenses is to inundate them with discovery requests. In fact, that's a common strategy in civil litigation for the most well-funded litigants—simply overwhelm the other party with motions, requests and legal filings that require an answer until the less well-funded respondent is forced to settle the case due to a lack of funds required to continue to participate in the legal process. Other burdens may also be imposed on the other party in the discovery process. For example, a request for information the other party does not want to expose for reasons unrelated to the case—information that may cause a hardship to the responding party if exposed—may present a difficult dilemma to the party forced to respond with sensitive information.

In order to most effectively maximize the impact of discovery requests, the approach to discovery needs to be logical, well-ordered, and architected with the end goal in mind. Deductive reasoning is the critical skill that often will determine the winner and loser in a civil case—and this skill can become most apparent during the discovery process.

With deductive reasoning, the guiding questions within the discovery process become obvious and universal regardless of the specifics of the case. Who is the best party to provide the information I need? Will that party willingly provide this information? Do they have an incentive or disincentive to provide? An incentive or disincentive to withhold? Are they a truly neutral party with no motivation related to the outcome of the case?

> " Deductive reasoning is the critical skill that
> often will determine the winner and loser in a
> civil case—and this skill can become most
> apparent during the discovery process."

The opposing party clearly has a disincentive to provide information that will damage their case. Of course, the Rules of Civil Procedure require responses and include various penalties for failing to properly respond. Yet, anyone who's ever been a party to a civil lawsuit will tell you there's plenty of gray area and room for interpretation when considering and responding to discovery requests. One well-worn path toward securing information of value to a lawsuit is to request this from third parties—preferably third parties who are evidently neutral. Neutrality can be questioned or compromised based on the third party's relationships with both the litigants—both professional and personal—as well as the third party's own potential liability that may result from disclosing certain information. Suffice it to say, when requesting discovery and examining responses from third parties, it's important to maintain a critical eye and apply deductive reasoning. Does this response make sense given the theory of the case and the evidence already in possession? Does this response appear to be complete or is there potential documentation or facts not yet disclosed? Based on the responses in-hand, what additional information should you request in a follow-up that may provide evidence that will support your case?

One fairly obvious discovery path that can sometimes be overlooked is the ability to obtain documentation from third parties outside of the discovery process. If a litigant is able to secure information from a third party without informing the opposing party in the lawsuit, the element of surprise can shift the dynamics of all the subsequent steps within the case. The other party may make damaging or outright false statements in depositions—statements known to be false due to the fact that the information is directly contradicted by information previously obtained outside the discovery process. Questions asked in depositions or interrogatories or documentation requested via the request for production process are all informed by previously obtained evidence, and related context, that the other side doesn't realize has been disclosed. The unaware party may be aware of the undisclosed facts—after all, the facts may be evidence of bad acts committed by this party—but not aware of the fact that the opponent in litigation knows this information and—most importantly - —has concrete evidence that can be admitted in a court of law.

> *One fairly obvious discovery path that can sometimes be overlooked is the ability to obtain documentation from third parties outside of the discovery process."*

An example of this phenomena is discovery requests related to tax returns in a trust dispute after the death of the trust's grantor. If there's a controversy regarding assets titled to the trust and the trustee—who may be a bad actor who absconded with funds—fails to produce trust tax returns in response to a discovery request, a logical alternative may be to request the relevant tax returns either from a related third party—such as a tax attorney or accountant—or directly from the Internal Revenue Service. In this example, a trust beneficiary can take two concurrent paths: continue to pressure the trustee to produce the relevant documentation via court orders such as a discovery request and even a motion to compel while also requesting this information directly from the third parties. The accountant or tax attorney will likely ask that the plaintiff request this documentation through the courts via a subpoena but, depending on their personal relationships with the beneficiary, the trustee, or even the deceased grantor of the trust, may discretely or even mistakenly provide insight as to whether or not going through the effort and expense of requesting this documentation from them is a worthwhile exercise. Another option is requesting this information directly from the IRS if you're authorized to receive it. In this example, the IRS's disclosure policy states that beneficiaries of a trust are authorized to receive tax returns and tax related documentation filed by the trust if the trust's grantor is deceased and the beneficiary is able to prove their status as a beneficiary (by providing a copy of the trust and verification of the beneficiary's own identify, for instance). This is a great example of the possibilities available to a litigant who's able to secure damaging information outside of the discovery process and, as a result, leverage the element of surprise for the remainder of the course of the lawsuit. The process of obtaining this information from the IRS, in this example, may be long, tedious, and require persistent effort but—beyond the element of surprise—it can also be cheaper than extensive and expansive litigation battles via the standard discovery process.

At its heart, the discovery process is focused on securing information from either the opposing party or a third-party witness in an effort to secure evidence that can be admitted in a court of law. The primary forms of discovery include the following:

- *Interrogatories:* written questions which require responses that include answers to the questions as well as the production of any relevant documentation. Responses need to be delivered within a defined time period (thirty days in many jurisdictions) and are considered under oath.
- *Requests for production:* documentation requests that allow the party receiving the information to examine and make copies of the information—responses are also considered under oath.
- *Depositions:* verbal questions asked of a party or witness to the case in-person. Depositions are generally taken in one of the attorney's offices, transcribed by a court reporter and—as with all other discovery material—considered under oath.
- *Admissions:* a request from one party to the other asking for a confirmation or denial of an alleged fact involved in the case—admissions are also considered under oath.

Each method of discovery presents pros and cons to the movant party. Interrogatories offer an opportunity to establish as evidence a set of certain facts but present the risk that the opposing side will both have time to contemplate their answer and, potentially ascertain your overall theory of the case based on your questions.

Requests for production are particularly helpful when seeking documentation that requires significant time and effort to examine—such as financial statements and related documentation—but presents the opposing party with the chance to overwhelm your legal team with documentation that may or may not be relevant. This may force the requesting party to spend time and, potentially, legal fees, to examine documentation that may not be relevant to the case.

Depositions provide the advantage of using the pressure associated with an in-person interview in combination with a well-prepared attorney (or self-represented litigant) trained in interrogation methods to identify inconsistencies in a witness's testimony that may not align with facts previously established or demonstrable facts that are supported by documentation previously obtained. Depositions are one of the most high-pressure situations in the civil legal process for a non-attorney—with the exception of testifying at trial. As such, depositions can often be used to test legal theories, explore various promising avenues of discovery, and establish a pattern of facts with a person who may or may not be prepared to testify or accustomed to participating in such a high-pressure environment. Of course, the opposing counsel may attempt to limit testimony—especially from potentially damaging witnesses—by claiming certain lines of questioning are outside the scope of the lawsuit. These are often the moments when the deductive reasoning skills of each legal team are most valuable and when—in many lawsuits—a case is won or lost.

The most effective discovery process includes tactical decisions that support an overall strategic approach to ensure the most damaging information is either introduced or excluded as evidence depending on the evidence's impact upon the entirety of your case. For example, a seasoned litigator for the plaintiff may serve interrogatories to the defendant that force the opposing party to make a declaration and use requests for production served upon third parties and depositions taken from third parties to establish the initial declaration is false and demonstrate that the opposing party has a history of failing to tell the truth. In another example, a plaintiff may discover a damaging fact buried in an avalanche of documentation provided as a result of a request for production for documentation. Subsequently, the plaintiff may ask a series of questions to the opposing party in a deposition, forcing the person to either make statements that are known as mistruths or voluntarily expose the damaging fact—a difficult choice for an unseasoned witness who may not be accustomed to thinking quickly in the moment. Concurrent discovery requests to multiple parties—for instance, the opposing party and a neutral third party, is another tactic that may present difficult choices to an opposing party who's a bad actor.

If a party fails to respond to a discovery request within the timeframe allotted by statute, the requesting party has the option to file an additional motion—known as a motion to compel—alerting the court to the party's failure to participate in the discovery process and asking the court to enforce the discovery request. Failure to comply with the original discovery request may be a legal strategy in itself. For example, a party may purposefully fail to respond to the initial request as a delay tactic in the hopes the opposing party may become sufficiently frustrated to drop the lawsuit—or as a method for increasing the legal bills of the requestor. In this scenario, the party requesting the information would be forced to pay additional legal fees to fund the effort by their lawyers to file the motion to compel and—in some instances—attend a hearing related to the discovery request.

The party who has been served the discovery request—the responding party—may fail to respond by simply ignoring the request or by stating that the discovery request is invalid given the particulars of the case. After all, any discovery request needs to be reasonably related to the issue of controversy. In either case, the requesting party can file a motion to compel seeking both confirmation from the court regarding the validity of the request and enforcement from the court in terms of response. The penalties for non-compliance to a court-ordered motion to compel include sanctions or even, potentially, a verdict ruling on behalf of the requesting party.

In order to secure sanctions with regard to a motion to compel, the requesting party can also file a motion for sanctions either at the same time as the motion to compel or subsequently. A motion for sanctions is an aggressive action with potentially serious consequences. As a result, there needs to be a demonstrable and egregious failing from the non-movant party to justify such an action. Common situations that meet this threshold include a failure to provide answers to interrogatories, failure to appear at your own deposition, failure to produce complete and true documentation or failure to provide complete answers either to interrogatories or questions within a deposition. Potential sanctions—depending on the situation—may include the court awarding reasonable legal fees to the injured party, striking the specific pleadings at issue, dismissing a case, or rendering a default judgment.

As a plaintiff, the goal is to ensure the evidence allows the litigant to meet all the elements of the initial complaint filed. From a strategic perspective, a plaintiff wants to use discovery as a means of confirming facts related to the elements of the complaint while minimizing or eliminating the various defenses of the opposing party with particular attention to the defenses referenced in their response to the initial complaint. A defendant also has the opportunity to use the discovery process to serve requests upon the opposing party as well as any relevant third parties. The goal of the defendant's discovery requests is to obtain evidence that either fortifies your own defense or invalidates the plaintiff's complaint.

> *From a strategic perspective, a plaintiff wants to use discovery as a means of confirming facts related to the elements of the complaint while minimizing or eliminating the various defenses of the opposing party with particular attention to the defenses referenced in their response to the initial complaint."*

Legal strategies with regard to the discovery process are as varied as the types of complaints brought to civil court. Given both parties have the right to request information and the obligation to respond to such requests, it may be helpful to consider the broad strategic goals of either a requestor or respondent. As a requester, the goals within the discovery process include the following:

- Obtain evidence that provides confirmation of a known fact or divulges a previously unknown fact that supports the case
- Write discovery requests with as much specificity as possible to eliminate the ability of the respondent to provide incomplete responses while still meeting the legal requirements of the request
- Alternatively, write discovery requests with as much generality as possible in an effort to force the respondent to provide more information (the opposing party's counsel may object to the lack of specificity)
- When possible, submit discovery requests on the same topic to multiple parties—for example, the opposing party and a third party—as a means of forcing the disclosure of evidence (the fact that a third party may disclose a known or suspected fact may force the opposing party to disclose a fact that is damaging.)
- Submit subsequent, stacking discovery requests that use previous responses to narrow the possible answers from the respondent and, by painting the opposing party in a corner, force the disclosure of damaging information

As a respondent, the goals within the discovery process include the following:

- Proactively respond with information that supports your case—either as a defendant or plaintiff—and invalidates the arguments of the opposing party
- Delay responses for a variety of reasons including increasing the legal cost and effort of the opposing party, deferring disclosure for as long as possible, or determin-

ing if a neutral third party will submit evidence that will necessitate your own disclosure

- Limit the response by interpreting the request as strict as is legally defensible
- Alternatively, respond with an overwhelming amount of information—for example, to a request for production—with both relevant and tangentially relevant documentation that will increase the amount of effort required to examine the response

The above strategies are simply examples of the countless iterations of available approaches that may be deployed within the discovery process depending on the facts, circumstances, and other particulars of a specific legal situation. The above suggestions, in some instances, may also apply to both the requester and the respondent. For example, the requester may use the strategy of overwhelming the opposing party with discovery requests as a means of increasing their legal expenses or even discouraging their continued participation with the lawsuit by demonstrating how difficult, time-consuming, and expensive the process may be. The respondent may use a similar tactic of overwhelming the requesting party with information and documentation to achieve the same goal of discouraging their continued pursuit of the case. There are pros and cons to each strategy and tactic that need to be considered as the client and legal team consider the best path toward successfully resolving the case in the most cost-effective manner possible (assuming the client's strategy is not to dedicate significant financial resources to the legal effort as a means of intimidating the opposing party).

Finally, it's important to remember that each party always has the ability to initiate discussions regarding a potential settlement at any time during the process. From the day the initial complaint is filed by the plaintiff to the moments immediately preceding a judge's ruling, there's an opportunity to negotiate a settlement agreement prior to judgment. As evidence is established during the discovery process, both plaintiff and defendant need to continually monitor the impact of the evidence upon the ability of the plaintiff to successfully meet the elements of the statute upon which the complaint was filed with an understanding that civil litigation is essentially a business transaction. The business case for each litigant will adjust—in terms of legal expenses compared to potential damages—as the discovery process unfolds. By closely monitoring the discovery process from the perspective of a business case, a wise litigant will be able to weigh the benefits and risks of both initiating settlement discussions and the value of settling the case at each particular moment in time.

> *The business case for each litigant will adjust— in terms of legal expenses compared to potential damages—as the discovery process unfolds."*

Attorney-Client Privilege in the Discovery Process

"Trust starts with truth and ends with truth."

—SANTOSH KALWAR

In some instances, the opposing party's lawyer presents one of the best opportunities to obtain valuable discovery. Attorney-client privilege —in any situation in which a lawyer is being asked to participate in the discovery process—will surface as an issue to be navigated and, likely, an obvious objection from the opposing party. The principle of attorney-client privilege holds that a client's communication with their attorney is confidential as a means of ensuring trust between attorney and client. In other words, attorney-client privilege exists to provide the client with the opportunity to confide in their lawyer and share all the facts and circumstances related to the lawsuit—even if such information reflects poorly on the client and is damaging to the case—without fear that the lawyer will divulge this information. In fact, if an attorney violates the attorney-client privilege without the explicit permission of their client—a client can waive this privilege if they want, in legal terms it's said that the client holds the privilege—the attorney may face significant repercussions such as disbarment or even criminal prosecution. The privilege is one of the oldest concepts in common law with the goal of ensuring the relationship between attorney and client allows for uncensored communications that will, in theory, result in the best legal representation for the client.

> *The privilege is one of the oldest concepts in common law with the goal of ensuring the relationship between attorney and client allows for uncensored communications that will, in theory, result in the best legal representation for the client."*

Yet, exceptions to the attorney-client privilege exist. The existence of an attorney-client relationship, the length of that relationship, and the scope of the legal engagement in terms of services rendered are—in most instances—fair game within the discovery process. For example, obtaining billing statements related to legal representation may provide insight into the timeframe when specific legal work was completed—for instance, the creation of a will or trust—that may be valuable in the overall context of a litigant's theory of the case. This type of information may not provide the smoking gun required to win a case but may provide invaluable context in terms of the relationships between parties and potential conflicts of interest.

Additionally, arguments debating whether or not an attorney-client relationship actually exists have been the basis for many disagreements resolved within the confines of the discovery process and related court intervention. The standard for the establishment of an attorney-client relationship can be confusing. The existence of an engagement agreement makes the relationship fairly obvious and indisputable. The behavior and actions of an attorney on behalf of a client—such as court appearances or filings—can also be fairly solid evidence that a relationship exists. It's in situations in which an attorney and client don't have a formal agreement and haven't taken any actions in any specific legal venue—but legal advice has been sought and provided—that the issue can be disputable and may become a subject of controversy within a legal proceeding. For example, is a phone call between an attorney and client that occurs before representation is agreed upon discoverable if the two parties never agree to work together? What are the factors that indicate representation and result in the protection of communication via the privilege? The subject matter of the discussion, the existence or non-existence of payment, or a history of legal representation between the two parties are examples of evidence that will be raised to either argue that a relationship of legal representation exists or doesn't exist. The wide variety of potential circumstances that may exist in combination with an abundance of case law make this area of the law potentially fraught but, if a litigant believes an attorney may have valuable information, it's sometimes worthwhile to dedicate the expense and time required to discover this information.

Other exceptions to the attorney-client privilege exist. The most common, and commonly discussed, is the crime or fraud exception. Communication related to any effort to enlist an attorney in the commission of a crime is discoverable and not covered under the privilege.

• • •

After all the legal wrangling, the opposing party and various third-party witnesses will eventually begin to respond to your discovery requests. The next step is to examine the information received in a systematic manner with an eye—as always—to leverage the discovery process to obtain evidence that strengthens your case.

Personality Disorders and the Discovery Process

"Every rascal is not a thief, but every thief is a rascal."

—ARISTOTLE

The civil courts are one of our nation's best venues for discovering and, in the best cases, rectifying some of society's most despicable and disgraceful acts. Of course, there are plenty of small claims issues heard in our country's civil courts. Disagreements with relatively small stakes from a financial perspective between two parties who can't seem to reach a compromise without the intervention of the legal system are heard in courtrooms every day. The civil justice system also hears countless lawsuits in which the stakes—financial, emotional, and even societal —are almost unimaginable and the outcomes impact the rest of the participants' lives.

The inherent conclusion one can draw from a court system flooded with heartbreaking stories that detail a wide variety of tragedies is that our society has no shortage of bad actors. This is a term used frequently by lawyers that—in my opinion—fails to convey the damage some of our society's most damaged individuals (and companies) commit. If a person is willing to steal money from a family member in an estate dispute, cheat a business partner out of their share of a joint endeavor's profits, or perpetrate all manner of loathsome acts that lead to divorce proceedings and child custody contests, some of those same people will not hesitate to continue their bad actions—even within a legal proceeding with the risk of significant penalties if these bad acts are discovered. The continuation of a bad act that originally led to a lawsuit may materialize as lies of both commission and omission, failure to produce damaging information, or any number of procedural violations that are technically illegal but—when viewed via the perspective of the original bad act—may not seem so flagrant to the bad actor. If a person commits a bad act that leads to a civil lawsuit, lying to prevent the disclosure of the original bad act can appear to be the most logical choice—particularly if the person fears disclosure may ultimately lead to criminal charges.

> " If a person is willing to steal money from a family member in an estate dispute, cheat a business partner out of their share of a joint endeavor's profits, or perpetrate all manner of loathsome acts that lead to divorce proceedings and child custody contests, some of those same people will not hesitate to continue their bad actions—even within a legal proceeding with the risk of significant penalties if these bad acts are discovered."

The problem is the good will of our society's good people who—thinking other people have a similar moral compass and general compassion for their fellow citizens—will tend to give the bad actors the benefit of the doubt. When you consider the fact that many lawsuits are disputes between individuals who know each other—or, at least, have some familiarity with each other—this natural tendency to believe the bad actor's lies, illogical explanations, or irrational excuses becomes even more influential. When good people interact with sociopaths, sometimes the civil court system is the only path available to successfully end the relationship or rectify the damage done by the sociopath.

In Martha Stout's excellent book titled *The Sociopath Next Door*[1], she states that one out of every twenty-five peo-

---

[1] https://www.amazon.com/Sociopath-Next-Door-Martha-Stout/dp/0767915828

ple are sociopaths. We can imagine our civil court systems in-fested with sociopaths! In the book, Martha Stout states that a sociopath's "defining trait is a lack of conscience." Her book details the behavior of a typical sociopath. The sociopath ma-nipulates people—for the benefit of the sociopath or simply for the amusement the sociopath receives from the act of ma-nipulation—takes advantage of the qualities most good people value—such as empathy, kindness, loyalty and honesty—and, most fiendishly—actively seeks people with such positive qual-ities in order to find useful targets for their manipulation.

> " *The problem is the good will of our society's good people who—thinking other people have a similar moral compass and general compassion for their fellow citizens—will tend to give the bad actors the benefit of the doubt.*"

Sociopathy is not a clinical diagnosis, but rather a term used to describe the characteristics of some people with antiso-cial personality disorder. *The Diagnostic and Statistical Manu-al, Fifth Edition* (DSM-5) published by the American Psychiatric Association outlines the characteristics required for a diagnosis of antisocial personality disorder. These characteristics include a failure to obey laws or norms, the frequent use of deception or manipulation, impulsivity, a disregard for the safety and securi-ty of others, a pattern of irresponsibility, and a lack of remorse for actions that impact others. These qualities in a person with an antisocial personality disorder can result in the significant impairment of their functioning within society.

Although not an official diagnosis of the DSM-5, the charac-teristics that define a sociopath are also found within the defi-nition of antisocial personality disorder. Additional sociopathic characteristics include unreliability, extreme egocentricity, lack of shame, and irrational thinking.

Individuals with narcissistic personality traits—and the good people whose lives become intertwined with a narcissist's—may also find themselves litigating their differences in civil court. The diagnosis of narcissistic personality disorder is different from antisocial personality disorder but the two conditions share a number of characteristics including a failure to feel empathy or guilt and an inability to meet society's expected norms. The defining traits of a narcissist are an inflated sense of self (often at the expense of others), and the associated egotistical behavior that is a result of this inflated sense of self and a sense of entitlement.

Not everyone who finds themselves in a civil courtroom is a sociopath, narcissist, or suffering from an antisocial personality disorder. In fact, most people are fair-minded individuals who think the court system is their best place to find some semblance of justice. Or at least a compromise that may be marginally acceptable. Yet, some people have conditions—whether diagnosed or not—that drive them to manipulate others, prevent them from feeling empathy or guilt, and nullify their ability to view a situation from another person's perspective and comprehend the damages their words and actions may inflict upon others.

People without a condition such as sociopathy, narcissism, or antisocial personality disorder are perfectly capable of lying in a deposition or offering misleading testimony in a trial or willfully withholding evidence and failing to respond properly to a request for production or attempting to tamper with witnesses or disregarding the Rules of Civil Procedure designed to ensure all litigants operate under the same rules of engagement. Here's the difference between people who commit bad acts and people who are inherently bad actors. For someone with a condition such as sociopathy, narcissism, or antisocial personality disorder this behavior comes much easier and without the nagging feelings of guilt and remorse that most of us feel when we commit a bad act—an act we know is wrong.

Odds are the other party in a lawsuit isn't a sociopath, or a narcissist. But, if they are, understand that the rules we've agreed to as a society—the moral code that consciously and unconsciously guides the behavior of all good people—doesn't apply to some of our fellow citizens. If you're in court because of the bad acts of someone in your life, there's the possibility that the behavior that led to the original disagreement will continue throughout the length of the lawsuit (and, potentially, beyond). Ensure your values endure—values can only be realized in challenging times. Expect the unexpected. And, most importantly, plan your legal strategy accordingly.

> *For someone with a condition such as sociopathy, narcissism, or antisocial personality disorder this behavior comes much easier and without the nagging feelings of guilt and remorse that most of us feel when we commit a bad act—an act we know is wrong."*

Phase Three:
Alternative Dispute
Resolution

(Mediation, Arbitration, and
Negotiated Settlement)

"Compromise is the best and cheapest lawyer."

— ROBERT LOUIS STEVENSON

The vast majority of civil cases aren't resolved in a courtroom. Instead of the courtroom drama and tension we've become accustomed to as a result of years of legal thrillers, most cases—particularly civil matters—are resolved via some combination of compromise, persuasion, and negotiation between the two parties and their respective legal counsels (when an attorney is engaged by a litigant) without the benefit or interference of a jury or bench trial (a trial heard solely by the judge). The various procedures that guide this process are defined as alternative dispute resolution and include mediation, arbitration, and negotiated settlement.

Given the prevalent use of the negotiated settlement, I've dedicated the next section in this book to detailing the typical format of a settlement agreement and exploring the various strategic decisions that need to be considered in settlement negotiations. Other alternative dispute resolution approaches—such as mediation or arbitration—may also include the use of a negotiated settlement agreement but—for the purposes of this section—I'll focus on the various particulars related to mediation and arbitration.

The commonalities between mediation and arbitration are the fact that both are more efficient in terms of time and legal expense when compared to traditional litigation, both rely on a neutral third-party to guide the process, both are considered informal approaches compared to traditional litigation, both provide the benefit of confidentiality in which proceedings do not become part of the public record, and both *may* be enforced by a court of law. The enforceable nature of alternative dispute resolution approaches such as mediation and arbitration need to be agreed to prior to commencing an alternative dispute resolution process.

Historically, mediation is a voluntary process in which participants are encouraged to collaborate to identify a potential compromise that will assuage both parties' concerns and alleviate the need to proceed with litigation. Prior to the mediation session, both parties agree to employ the services of a mediator to assist with the process. Most states have laws that govern the actions of mediators but there isn't a standard governing body—from a federal perspective—that provides unified guidance regarding mediator qualifications. As such, individuals in any state can qualify to practice in private settings—such as serving as a mediator in a civil law dispute—without any state license or certification. Given the prevalence of the use of mediation services, most lawyers will have individual mediators who they trust as a neutral party to assist with the collaboration required to reach an agreement via mediation.

The role of the mediator is, primarily, to encourage discussion and compromise with the goal of reaching an agreement that is amenable to both parties. Mediators will often tout their success rates with resolving disputes through the mediation process in the sales and marketing efforts associated with their service. As a result, mediators have an incentive to find common ground between the parties both as a means of fulfilling their primary role and also to maintain the high success rate that allows them to market their services.

The best mediators will approach a mediation session with a framework to proceed while maintaining the flexibility to adjust based on the circumstances. The mediation session typically begins with both parties making a commitment to the process and a promise to act in good faith to seek a resolution. Often, each party will begin with a statement of the situation from their perspective including comments related to the type of relief sought through the mediation process. The mediation process doesn't require the participation of legal counsel but, particularly with regard to complex legal situations, including your attorney in the process can both help to identify and negotiate a potential settlement agreement and increase your lawyer's understanding of the circumstances of the situation. Information gained via the mediation process—even when the process doesn't result in a negotiated settlement —may be valuable if the case proceeds without a settlement.

Experienced mediators state that the process is well-suited for cases where one party or the other will benefit significantly, in terms of saved time and money, from the early resolution of a case. Additionally, exploring a potential resolution within the confines of mediation earlier, rather than later, in the course of a lawsuit can also lead to more successful outcomes with mediation due to the fact that the parties haven't already invested resources in the litigation effort. Conversely, in cases where an early settlement may result in additional claims from other parties—such as a medical malpractice lawsuit in which other harmed parties may also have similar complaints—are not good candidates for mediation given the defendant's disincentive to expedite settling the case.

From a process perspective, mediation can serve as a tool to shorten and expedite the churn—in the form of demands and responses—associated with negotiation. On a related note, mediation can provide a similar benefit by mitigating the emotional impact of the negotiation process when compared to settlement discussions periodically explored over the course of a lawsuit. The lack of formality within the mediation process also leads to the primary benefit of mediation—the opportunity for both parties to learn the true motivations of the opposing party regarding the matter. While certainly not a substitute for the legal discovery process, mediation provides participants with a different, and arguably more important, form of discovery: the chance to learn the perspective of the opposing party. Which items are absolutely non-negotiable and which items present an opportunity to work toward a compromise? By understanding the importance the opposing party attaches to the various components that would be included—presumably—in a negotiated settlement, the parties are able to deliberately advance toward a resolution that—while not either party's vision of success—may provide a sufficient level of satisfaction.

> *By understanding the importance the opposing party attaches to the various components that would be included—presumably—in a negotiated settlement, the parties are able to deliberately advance toward a resolution that—while not either party's vision of success—may provide a sufficient level of satisfaction."*

In some situations, a judge will order the two parties to participate in a mediation session to seek a resolution. Divorce and child custody cases often include court ordered mediation but judges have used their discretion to order mediation in a wide variety of types of cases. Whether mediation is scheduled as a result of a court order or an independent agreement between the two parties, the central tenets of mediation—voluntary and uncoerced—remains. Even within a court-ordered mediation, the process and—most importantly - —the spirit of the process as described above endures.

While arbitration may share a number of important qualities with mediation and the same overarching goal of an expedited and cost-effective resolution, arbitration differs from mediation in a number of critical respects. The primary difference is related to the method parties may find themselves in an arbitration hearing compared to mediation. While arbitration may be entered into voluntarily by parties who agree to abide by an arbitrator's final decision, many parties find themselves in an arbitration hearing due to the widespread adoption of arbitration clauses in commercial contracts.

Unlike mediation requirements, arbitration is included as a clause in contracts as the required path available to resolve any disputes related to the relevant contract. For example, arbitration clauses are often included in employment contracts, real estate contracts, consumer goods contracts, the terms and conditions of software contracts, and a wide variety of other commercial contracts.

By entering into a contract with an arbitration clause, the parties are essentially stating that any dispute related to the contract—and in some circumstances, by extension, the use of the related product or service—will be resolved via arbitration rather than the standard civil trial process. The practice of including arbitration clauses in commercial contracts, while widespread, is controversial due to the fact that some consumers may unknowingly enter a contract with an arbitration clause—for example, a contract for a credit card—that essentially restricts their ability to access the standard litigation process. Including arbitration clauses in employment contracts has also been widely adopted and criticized for the same reason. In order to accept the job offer, a prospective employee may be required to sign an employment contract with an arbitration clause—essentially forcing the prospective employee to limit their access to the civil court system in exchange for employment.

Arbitration is less formal than traditional litigation and more formal than mediation. As discussed, in mediation the mediator collaborates with both parties to jointly seek a resolution. In arbitration, the arbitrator's role shares many similarities with the judge's role in civil litigation. The arbitration process begins when one party sends a demand letter insisting upon arbitration—often as a result of the arbitration clause in a contract. Once established, the parties negotiate to identify and engage the services of an arbitrator who's agreeable to each party.

At this point, the arbitration process includes a preliminary hearing (or hearings) in which both parties convey the substantive issues of the case to the arbitrator as well as exchange documentation and witness lists. This step of the arbitration process may look vaguely similar to the discovery process within traditional litigation but the preliminary hearing(s) in arbitration is not subject to the rules and procedures of civil law. The arbitration process does not include formal discovery requests or motion practice. The process and the scope—in terms of documentation and witnesses—are agreed upon by the parties with guidance provided by the arbitrator. This process is also informed by presumptively discoverable documents as outlined by a variety of governing bodies. For example, the American Arbitration Association maintains an "Initial Discovery Protocols for Employment Arbitration Cases" and the Financial Industry Regulatory Authority (FINRA) maintains a "Discovery Guide" for consumer cases.

Once information is exchanged, hearings are scheduled to allow the parties to present evidence and witness testimony to the arbitrator. After listening to each party's case and reviewing the relevant evidence, the arbitrator will render a decision and close the case. The arbitrator's discretion allows for a decision to include financial damages or a ruling that requires one party to either begin or cease a defined action. In many cases, the results of the arbitration are binding—meaning final and enforceable. The binding nature as often outlined in arbitration clauses included in commercial contracts is a primary reason for the criticism. Alternatively, parties may decide to proceed through a non-binding arbitration. In this case, the arbitration process is the same as outlined above including a decision from the arbitrator. In non-binding arbitration, one or both parties may reject the results of the arbitration process and proceed to trial through the traditional civil litigation process. In this case, the results of the arbitration may serve as a launching point for additional discussions toward a negotiated settlement within traditional litigation (or may not be referenced as the case proceeds).

Often discussed from the perspective of a contractually obligated process, the arbitration process is also available as a voluntary alternative dispute resolution process to any party considering litigation or currently involved in a lawsuit interested in resolving a dispute outside the confines of traditional litigation—if the other party agrees to participate.

Settlement Agreements

"Victor and vanquished never unite in substantial agreement."

—TACITUS

Given the complexities of the civil justice system and the wide variety of the types of lawsuits heard by civil courts, it's difficult to determine the exact rate at which civil complaints are settled without a trial. Estimates vary based on the parameters of the study but it's safe to say the vast majority of civil cases reach a settlement between the parties prior to a judge's ruling in a trial. In fact, if you survey the various studies available on the topic you'll find that between 82 percent and 97 percent of civil lawsuits are resolved by a settlement agreement reached either independently between the two parties or as a result of participation within an alternative dispute resolution process.

Theoretically, a settlement agreement can offer benefits to both parties of a lawsuit as well as the civil courts themselves. Judges will often encourage litigants to explore potential paths toward settlement as a means of both resolving the matter quickly and alleviating the perpetually crowded court dockets. If a lawsuit can be dismissed via settlement agreement, that's one less complaint that the courts will need to manage on their calendar.

> *In fact, if you survey the various studies available on the topic you'll find that between 82 percent and 97 percent of civil lawsuits are resolved by a settlement agreement reached either independently between the two parties or as a result of participation within an alternative dispute resolution process."*

The potential benefits to the litigants include a potential reduction in legal fees and court costs, the ability to allocate time to other pursuits beyond the lawsuit, the reduction of stress associated with participating in the civil action, and the opportunity costs associated in terms of both time and money attached to continued participation in the lawsuit. Of course, every legal situation is different and, as a result, the benefits of negotiating a settlement agreement are often not clear to or equally realized by each litigant.

The scope of a settlement agreement is to be negotiated between the two parties and, when relevant, their lawyers. As a result, creativity is a critical skill in discussions regarding a potential settlement agreement similar to any other negotiation. Settlement agreements are enforceable contracts and, as such, require specificity in order to ensure the agreement is enforceable. In general, the standard settlement agreement includes the following components:

- *Definition of parties:* Typically, the settlement agreement references the two parties who are litigants within the lawsuit. This issue can become complicated and contentious when you consider the legal term "capacity" in reference to legal parties. For example, a settlement agreement may be executed between two parties both in their individual capacity. If the agreement does not contemplate one of the individuals who may also be operating in a different capacity (or, at least, argued to be operating in a different capacity), this may present issues post-execution. For example, the original lawsuit may include an individual operating in their individual capacity as a party to the lawsuit. If this same individual is also operating in a different capacity, such as a trustee with fiduciary duties, this may provide justification for the opposing party to continue to pursue the issue by filing a separate lawsuit against the same individual in their capacity as trustee.

  Definitions may seem straightforward—even boilerplate—but it's important to consider all possibilities when executing a settlement agreement. The same concept of broad inclusion may also apply to situations in which there are multiple defendants and/or plaintiffs, though each party may have a different perspective on the circumstances of the current lawsuit and varying degrees of appetite for participation in a settlement agreement.

- *Scope of the settlement:* The crux of the settlement agreement is the scope of the settlement detailing the particulars regarding the agreement between the two parties. For example, in some instances one or both parties may seek to ensure the settlement agreement resolves all current and potential future disputes that have surfaced or could arise in the future with regard to the controversy at issue. By contrast, some litigants want to employ a settlement agreement to resolve a narrow set of issues and retain the ability to further pursue related matters via the civil court in the future. The scope of the settlement agreement needs to provide clarity and specifics at a level of detail sufficient to ensure the intention of the agreement is clear to a future court if the issue is brought before a court post-execution.

- *Payment (including any applicable legal costs):* The foundation of most settlement agreements is a promise by one party or parties to pay an agreed-upon sum to another party or parties in exchange for the other party agreeing to cease pursuit of the matter in civil court. Settlement agreements often consider a wide variety of other clauses as components of the negotiated settlement but, at its heart, the agreement strongly relies on a cash payment in many instances. The party or parties who've agreed to pay, the party or parties who've agreed to settle in exchange for payment, the payment amount, the schedule of the payment, contingencies for late payment such as an agreed-upon interest rate, or details related to enforcement in the event of lack of payment and any other relevant details (such as payment currency, tax considerations, etc.) need to be outlined in the settlement agreement in order to ensure a valid and enforceable contract.

- *Confidentiality:* Settlement agreements don't inherently need to be treated as confidential by the parties to the agreement. As a result, it can be helpful in negotiations to treat this as simply another provision that can be negotiated. In some circumstances, confidentiality is a critical provision—to either one or both parties. Concurrently, there are plenty of examples where the inclusion of a confidentiality provision has done a disservice to one of the parties to a settlement agreement. This issue has gotten increased visibility in both the legal industry and the culture at large as parties—particularly plaintiffs in lawsuits accusing powerful individuals of despicable acts—have realized that the inclusion of a confidentiality clause has allowed these bad actors to continue their egregious behavior and restricted individuals with first-hand knowledge of bad acts from speaking. As with any provision included in a negotiation, assessing the level of importance of a confidentiality clause—or even whether or not the clause is important at all—allows your legal counsel to plan accordingly and advocate on your behalf.

- *Governing law and jurisdiction:* Including clauses that explicitly outline the law and court system that govern the settlement agreement is invaluable guidance in the event a settlement agreement is later challenged by one of the parties. For example, a settlement agreement that includes a governing law and jurisdiction clause will explicitly declare a specific state as the governing law and specific jurisdiction (such as the state court) as the law and jurisdiction which the settlement agreement is subject to in the event of any future controversy.

- *Execution:* With the goal of ensuring the enforceability of a settlement agreement, verifying the fact that the signatories of the agreement have the authority to enter into such a contract is crucial. A good example is the need to determine the authority to execute a contract of an individual executing on behalf of a corporation when the corporation is a party entering the settlement agreement.

Other Considerations in a Settlement Agreement

A general and mutual release clause is also a common clause included in settlement agreements. The purpose of this clause is to declare that both parties are absolving each other of liability for any claims—*known or unknown*. Despite the fact that this clause is often included as standard, boiler-plate language in settlement agreements, the inclusion of this type of clause needs to be carefully considered. The execution of a settlement agreement which includes this clause effectively eliminates both parties' ability to resolve any further disputes via the legal system. In many civil cases, this is included to support the concept of finality within a settlement agreement. Once signed, the dispute is over. This is certainly the principle behind the execution of a settlement agreement but there are circumstances that allow for one party to dispute the validity of a settlement agreement—for example, if one party willfully withheld damaging evidence that, upon discovery, would have likely precluded the other party from entering into the agreement. With this in mind, understanding the circumstances of the legal controversy and assessing the likelihood that potentially damaging information may be brought to light in the future can inform the necessity of including this clause in a settlement agreement.

Another common clause within settlement agreements is a "no admission of liability" provision—often insisted upon by defendants who agree to make a payment in exchange for the plaintiff agreeing to settle the lawsuit without the further pursuit of their claim. Defendants will often insist on the inclusion of this provision as a protective measure—in addition, at times, with a confidentiality clause—if they're concerned about the circumstances of a civil lawsuit becoming the focus of a criminal prosecution.

When considering the development of legal settlement agreements, hope is not an option. A settlement agreement is fundamentally a contract and—as with all contracts—the terms and provisions of the settlement agreement need to be negotiated to align with the goals of each party. For example, one party may insist on a confidentiality clause—and may even be willing to pay an additional sum of money to ensure its inclusion. Another litigant may only care about the finality of the issue—they just want this legal hassle out of their lives—and, as a result insist on a general and mutual release with a scope that includes all known and unknown claims. They may even outline all the possible claims within the body of the settlement agreement to ensure there isn't any ambiguity with regard to the matter. "Expect the worst, plan for the best" is a good motto for the development of a settlement agreement.

> *A settlement agreement is fundamentally a contract and—as with all contracts—the terms and provisions of the settlement agreement need to be negotiated to align with the goals of each party."*

Once discussions have begun regarding a settlement agreement, it's important for both parties to understand the potential finality of entering such a contract and assessing the pros and cons of executing a settlement agreement compared to continuing to pursue or fight a legal claim. In the ideal world, the legal process will result in perfect communication and perfect information—a situation in which both parties are operating with the same set of facts. The reality is a world of perfect information does not exist and—in most lawsuits—one party (often, but not always, the defendant) will hold an advantage regarding the availability of information or the interpretation of available information. Settlement agreements have a well-understood role to play in resolving disputes between two parties in an expeditious manner but they've also historically been used to restrict information, suppress the discovery of damaging information and, ultimately, impede the pursuit of justice.

Once the two parties have executed a settlement agreement, a motion needs to be introduced to the court asking the judge to approve of the settlement. The court's approval of a settlement agreement makes the contract binding and enforceable. In other words, the issue is effectively resolved from the court's perspective and can no longer be litigated. There are some extreme situations where a settlement agreement can be challenged and an issue can be revisited in civil courts but the court's strong bias—supported by significant case law—is that settlement agreements are final. If you find yourself contemplating the execution of a settlement agreement, understand that in all likelihood the execution of this agreement will end this matter forever. Act accordingly. Don't be bullied into signing a settlement agreement. Don't allow any artificial time constraints to force you to sign a settlement agreement. Contemplate the business case of a settlement agreement compared to continued pursuit in terms of time and legal expenses. If there's a payment offered, how does that compare to potential future damages if you continue your case? If you're offering compensation, does the fact that the case will no longer be pursued justify the expense? Most importantly, does the settlement agreement offer the justice you're seeking? Or at least a version of justice sufficient to move on with your life?

> Settlement agreements have a well-understood role to play in resolving disputes between two parties in an expeditious manner but they've also historically been used to restrict information, suppress the discovery of damaging information and, ultimately, impede the pursuit of justice."

A Note about Multiple Lawsuits

"Fall seven times, stand up eight."

—JAPANESE PROVERB

Civil law allows the filing of multiple complaints by the same plaintiff against the same defendant either as multiple lawsuits or a single, combined lawsuit. This presents both a risk and an opportunity to the plaintiff.

In the ideal situation for the plaintiff, the bad actions are well understood and the plaintiff has possession, or has a clear path to obtain possession, of the evidence required to meet the burden of proof. When the defendant is suspected of bad actions but the details of such potential actions is not well understood, a plaintiff may decide to file multiple complaints simultaneously in order to widen the scope of the discovery process. This increases the plaintiff's potential opportunity to obtain incriminating evidence, but also increases the defense's argument that the lawsuit, and each individual complaint, is frivolous. A good defense attorney will identify this strategy as a so-called "fishing expedition" and will argue accordingly. This presents significant risk to the plaintiff of having a valid complaint tarnished by its association with an ill-defined complaint. Additionally, failing to meet the burden of a filed complaint may reduce the plaintiff's ability to further pursue the matter in the future—depending on how the complaint is resolved.

Yet, there are situations where the filing of multiple complaints simultaneously may be a useful and practical legal strategy. This may allow the plaintiff a longer time period to gather intelligence—ideally, from a third party, which may support one or all of the multiple complaints. A plaintiff with significant capital may also deploy this strategy as a means of forcing the defendant to spend additional money to defend themselves on multiple fronts. Alternatively, a well-financed plaintiff may name multiple defendants in a single complaint—or file separate complaints regarding the same matter against multiple defendants—as a legal strategy and means of achieving larger goals such as increasing the available pool for damages recovery or fracturing the relationship between potential defendants.

Initiating civil proceedings with a single complaint can be fraught with complications and expenses. A wise plaintiff needs to consider the potential implications of filing multiple complaints in a single lawsuit—or multiple simultaneous lawsuits against different parties—to ensure this decision is based in logical strategic and legal thinking without allowing emotions to compromise your judgment.

Class Action Lawsuits

> *"No member of a crew is praised for the*
> *rugged individuality of his rowing."*
>
> — RALPH WALDO EMERSON

The movie *Erin Brockovich*—in which Julia Roberts played the lead role in the fight against PG&E and the company's negligence in releasing harmful chemicals into the groundwater supply of the town of Hinkley, California—brought the concept of class action lawsuits to the attention of a wider audience. Yet, class action lawsuits have a long history—particularly in the United States—and have, at times, been at the center of many of the country's most controversial legal issues.

The legal definition of a class action lawsuit is the filing of a complaint in civil court on behalf of a "class" against a party that has damaged each party that comprises the plaintiff's class. Such class actions often garner significant media coverage due to the types of issues underlying these cases and, in some cases, the extremely large awards of damages. Examples of recent class action lawsuits have included complaints regarding the racial profiling practices of police departments, the hiring practices of corporations based on gender, racial and gender discrimination practices, Internet privacy rights, and telecommunications surveillance.

If you think your case may qualify for class action status, it may be worth exploring that avenue. The pursuit of resolution via class action lawsuit is, by definition, infinitely more complicated than the standard single party complaint. Class action lawsuits, obviously, include the participation of many individuals that comprise the group and, as a result, each individual's particular facts and circumstances need to be taken into consideration. In effect, a plaintiff is tying their grievance to the unique situations of each of the other members of the class when the collected grievance conveys a larger pattern of harm.

Due to this complexity, a group of specialists has emerged as class action plaintiff and defense attorneys. As a result, class action lawsuits are a highly specialized area of the law and require the assistance of an attorney who specializes in class actions. This is not an area of the law suitable for self-represented litigants. This area of the law is far from typical and, as such, outside the purview of this text. Yet, it's critical that a plaintiff determine the best course of action—filing as an individual or as a member of a class—based on the same factors that should be considered with every potential legal action. What is your grievance and how do you make the strongest argument? How can you obtain the evidence required to meet your burden of proof? What is the estimated return on investment for pursuing this matter? In what timeframe can you expect a successful resolution? What are the potential advantages, in terms of both time and money, and how should you weigh those advantages against the potential payback if the lawsuit is successful?

> *In effect, a plaintiff is tying their grievance to the unique situations of each of the other members of the class when the collected grievance conveys a larger pattern of harm."*

A savvy plaintiff can use these questions as guideposts to determine the best path forward when participation in a class action lawsuit is a potential option.

Phase Four:
Trial Preparation and Execution

"Knowledge is the process of piling up facts;
wisdom lies in their simplification."

— MARTIN H. FISCHER

T he reality of trial preparation, in most civil lawsuits, is related to the threat of a trial as much as actually preparing for a trial. Civil attorneys understand this dynamic very well and will use the typical activities that are components of preparing for a trial as levers to be used when negotiating a settlement. In this way, trial preparation is an activity that should begin the day a complaint is filed and maintained through the legal journey. After all, you never know when the opposing party will seek to initiate settlement discussions. It's best to be prepared at any time to articulate the strength of your case with specifics to ensure you're ready to maximize your negotiating position.

Maintaining a level of constant preparation is an approach a savvy litigant can adopt to ensure he or she is prepared for any eventuality. Attention to the project management required to effectively litigate a matter is essential but balancing the daily requirements with long-term trial preparation can often be the difference between a well-argued case and a winning case. Managing the various documents associated with a civil lawsuit including potential evidence as well as the myriad legal filings by both parties, maintaining a diary to record every interaction of the various parties involved in the lawsuit and recording details related to evidence—existing and potential—and legal theories that may apply to the case are all time-consuming but well-worth the effort. These are all activities a legal team would perform on your behalf, if you had decided to hire an attorney, but deciding to self-represent also means deciding that these activities are now your responsibility. This level of participation will allow a savvy litigant to continually understand the current state of the lawsuit and be prepared for any settlement discussions that may arise or eventual trial, if the case proceeds to that stage. A complete record of the legal proceedings will also help you to (somewhat) alleviate the stress associated with the unknown that is inherently a component of the civil justice process and communicate to your lawyer that this legal matter is important to you by virtue of being informed of the situation. If, at some point in the future, you decide to engage the services of an attorney this approach will allow the newly-hired lawyer to quickly get up to speed on the issues at controversy in your case and the actions and counteractions that have previously transpired. Even if a trial is not likely to be in your future, preparing as if it's inevitable serves a variety of valuable purposes.

In the event a case doesn't settle prior to trial, the priorities in trial preparation include the following:

- Effectively communicating your case to the court with a compelling narrative detailing the facts, circumstances, and applicable case law

- Conveying to the court the elements required to meet the burden associated with the complaint and detailing how each element is met within the compelling narrative

This is the plaintiff's goal. If you're a defendant, your goal is to convey the fact that the plaintiff hasn't sufficiently met the elements of the complaint.

- Ensuring any components of your case that may provide an avenue for appeal are introduced and included within the court record

  Any potential appeal needs to be based on an issue that was presented to the court (an appeal can't be based on new evidence). As a result, savvy litigators will ensure appealable items are included in the court record.

The most important component of trial preparation is a business case review in the form of comparing risk and reward in the event the matter proceeds through trial and results in a judicial ruling. Comparing the potential damages with the potential costs of litigating a trial provides an important perspective and informs a party's decision to either settle or proceed to trial. This simple calculation is the story behind the statistics related to the percentage of cases that settle prior to trial. Considering your own financial resources as well as the resources of the opposing party, the sunk legal costs/fees and potential future legal expenses, the merits of the case, any evidentiary or discovery issues, the time required to proceed, and the impact of proceeding on the relationship of the parties are all factors that may impact whether a case goes to trial or not.

Prior to trial, there are often pre-trial motions—for example, examining issues related to either the admissibility of evidence or the applicability of case law—that may inform both potential settlement discussions and/or trial preparation. The pre-trial motions are critical milestones where a judge's ruling can influence the calculus of the two parties and result in either a settlement agreement or proceeding to trial. For example, one party may file a motion to compel to request that the court require the defendant (or a third party witness) respond appropriately and completely to a discovery request or file a motion to exclude or admit specific evidence based on applicable case law. The judge's ruling on such a motion—whether or not to require a response to a discovery request or whether or not to admit or exclude evidence—can oftentimes have a significant impact on both parties' ability to argue their case. The impact of such pre-trial hearings is to effectively narrow the parameters of the case which will inform the arguments of each party and, most interestingly, provide a window into the judge's thinking with regard to each party's specific arguments. This is obviously true with regard to the issue argued during the pre-trial hearing but a judge's opinion regarding each party's overall theory of the case can also be intuited as a result of pre-trial hearings. It also explains the phenomena of "courtroom steps settlement agreements." This term often refers to agreements reached immediately prior to, or during, a trial but can also refer to agreements reached as a result of a pre-trial hearing ruling.

Once pre-trial hearings are concluded and a trial is scheduled, the trial proceeds based on the standard procedures as outlined by the Rules of Civil Procedure. The steps of a civil trial include the following:

- Opening statements
- Witness testimony and cross-examination
- Closing arguments
- Jury instruction, deliberation, and verdict (or simply finding, which is the equivalent of verdict, in a bench trial)

Opening statements present an opportunity for both parties to outline the particulars of the case and share a roadmap for the remainder of the trial. Opening statements are limited to known facts and cannot be argumentative in nature. In terms of cadence, the plaintiff has the opportunity to present their opening statement prior to the defendant's opening statement. The defendant can choose to either present an opening statement immediately after the plaintiff, prior to the introduction of any evidence or witness testimony, or can choose to wait until the plaintiff has concluded the presentation of their case.

The phase of the trial that includes witness testimony, and cross-examination of that testimony, is the method for introducing evidence to the proceedings. This represents the bulk of the trial and is the plaintiff's opportunity to ensure they've met each of the various elements associated with the complaint filed. For the defendant, this is an opportunity to present their side of the story and—critically—seek to ensure the plaintiff fails to meet the various elements of their complaint. Each party can call various witnesses to testify and—once questioning is complete—the opposing party has the opportunity to cross-examine the witness (meaning ask their own questions of the witness). In this phase of the trial, both litigants will seek to use legal procedure to proactively introduce evidence—through the questioning of witnesses—that supports their case while limiting the introduction of evidence—through objections to the opposing side's questioning—that may harm their case.

The most common forms of objections include hearsay, leading the witness, and relevancy. Hearsay is information received from other people. Given the fact that hearsay can't be refuted, hearsay is inadmissible in court. The objection related to leading the witness concerns the manner in which the attorney/self-represented litigant is asking questions of the witness. An attorney/self-represented litigant is not allowed to testify on behalf of a witness—the testimony needs to emanate from the witness. An objection to relevance is an objection stating the question is not related to the controversy at issue in the trial. This is a particularly thorny objection given the legal disputes related to the introduction, or restriction, of evidence in a proceeding. A question may, on its surface, appear relevant but—if the evidence related to the question has been ruled inadmissible—the judge's perspective of the question may not be so straightforward. A number of other types of objections are available including objections to vague questions, compound questions, argumentative questions, or objections to questions without a foundation (this is related to an attempt to introduce evidence not previously established through a question posed to a witness).

After each objection, the judge will issue a ruling—either sustained or overruled—regarding the particular question or line of questioning. If the judge sustains an objection, this means the judge agrees with the objection and the question is disallowed. Conversely, if the judge overrules the objection, then the judge disagrees with the objection and the question is allowed.

The closing arguments of a trial present both parties with the opportunity to summarize the factual evidence and witness testimony presented during the trial and convince the jury, or judge in a bench trial, to view the evidence from your perspective. The critical difference between the opening and closing arguments is—in closing arguments—attorneys/self-represented litigants are allowed to go beyond the presentation of facts and argue the merits of the case. The closing argument is the moment when a litigant's abilities as a storyteller are permitted. In this final stage, each party uses their creativity to develop a narrative that convinces the judge or jury of the viability of their case. In closing arguments, litigants still must rely strictly on the facts previously presented during the course of the proceedings but are generally permitted to be more expressive and expansive. Additionally, the closing argument provides an opportunity to clarify any information previously presented—to effectively educate the judge and jury—as well as address any unfavorable facts that may bolster the opposing party's case. Finally, the closing argument is the final opportunity to establish credibility with the judge and jury—a goal that should be pursued through the entirety of the trial.

Once closing arguments are complete, each party has made their case and the decision rests with the judge and jury. In a jury trial, the jury will receive instructions from the judge and be asked to deliberate and return a verdict. In a bench trial, arguments are only heard by a judge who is solely responsible for rendering a finding (the equivalent of a jury verdict).

After closing arguments, both parties are forced to wait for the judge or jury to deliberate and return a verdict (or finding). Of course, even at this late hour, the parties can still negotiate a settlement agreement. Settlements can be reached at any time after a complaint is filed including before the trial, during the course of the trial, during deliberation, or even after a verdict is rendered (though this is a rare occurrence).

Bench or Jury Trial

"I was married to a judge. I should have asked for a jury."

— GROUCHO MARX

When a trial is heard and decided upon solely by the judge, this is referred to as a bench trial. Alternatively, a jury trial is heard by a group of individuals from the jurisdiction or community who are tasked with rendering a verdict informed by instructions from the judge regarding specific legal concepts that may apply to the case.

The rules governing whether or not a trial is heard by a judge or jury differ but, in most states, the default is a bench trial unless one of the parties requests a jury trial. The strategic decision between bench and jury trial is informed by many factors including your understanding of the assigned judge's reputation and legal perspective as well as the typical profile of a jury in the jurisdiction. This is an area of civil litigation where practicing attorneys have a significant advantage compared to self-represented litigants given their experience with litigation, in general, and litigating cases in front of specific judges, in particular. An experienced attorney practicing in a specific jurisdiction will have an understanding of how most of the judges in that jurisdiction may view the overall narrative of your case—either as a result of previous appearances in front of the judge or by reputation. Additionally, attorneys will also have informed opinions regarding how the typical jury within the jurisdiction may react to your case based on previous jury trial experience and a familiarity with the community as a whole—another advantage experienced attorneys have compared to self-represented litigants.

> *An experienced attorney practicing in a specific jurisdiction will have an understanding of how most of the judges in that jurisdiction may view the overall narrative of your case—either as a result of previous appearances in front of the judge or by reputation."*

The traditional view of this strategic decision holds that parties should request a jury trial when their case includes an emotional appeal while parties with a case based on complex legal theories are better served by a bench trial. Additionally, juries tend to be more sympathetic to injured plaintiffs, are more likely to get confused by technical legal concepts, and have a tendency to issue verdicts with high damage and punitive damage awards compared to judges. On the other hand, judges are less easily swayed by emotional appeal, more apt to avoid confusion with technical legal concepts, and hesitant to award high damage amounts or punitive damages.

Of course, there are exceptions to this country lawyer view of the jury versus bench trial question. The individuals who comprise the jury and the individual parties to the lawsuit will naturally either strengthen or weaken any potential emotional appeal associated with the case. Additionally, even the most experienced judges can become confused about technical legal concepts. This is particularly true in areas of the law that the judge is not familiar with. Judges often hear cases in many different areas of the law—but the complexity of the law, and the frequency in which a specific judge hears a case that includes a specific legal concept, results in plenty of judges who aren't the legal experts we envision. This is why it's a truism that a good lawyer will educate a judge or jury not only on the specific merits of their case but also on the legal concepts and case law that apply.

When considering whether a bench or jury trial would be best for your specific case, the decision can be said to be more art than science. Does your case include an emotional appeal that may result in sympathy from at least one member of the jury? Remember, it's easier to create sympathy with one member of a twelve-person jury than a single judge who may be less inclined to provide a sympathetic ear due to a career on the bench of listening to people's hardships. Do you think the legal theory and concepts at the heart of your case can be effectively explained to a jury likely composed of members with limited, if any, experience within the civil justice system? Would the typical member of your community view your story favorably or be skeptical of your experience? And, most importantly, are you willing to risk the outcome of the lawsuit to the unpredictable and potentially fickle opinion of a single person—even if that person is a judge?

Phase Five:
Judicial Rulings and
the Appeals Process

*"Independence means you decide according
to the law and the facts."*

— JUSTICE STEPHEN BREYER

Judicial Rulings

Once a verdict is rendered by the jury—or a finding by the judge—the next step in the civil justice process is the judge's ruling. In the example of a jury trial, a trial will "find" in favor of either the plaintiff or defendant and specify any financial damages due to the plaintiff from the defendant (this is usually determined after a separate hearing related to damages). Additionally, the jury will also provide the court with a decision related to any counterclaims filed by the defendant—for example, a motion for award of legal fees.

There are two types of damages within the purview of civil lawsuits: compensatory damages and punitive damages. Compensatory damages are damages to reimburse an injured plaintiff. In a personal injury lawsuit as a result of an automobile accident, for example, compensatory damages could range from the damage to the plaintiff's automobile or the value for replacing a car that is not salvageable, medical bills as a result of the plaintiff's injuries, lost wages as a result of the plaintiff's inability to perform in their job or reduction in the plaintiff's future ability or capacity to work, and emotional distress as a result of the accident. The purpose of compensatory damages is to *compensate* the plaintiff for the damage caused as a result of the accident. In contrast, punitive damages are designed to serve as both a punishment for bad actions and a deterrence, for other actors within society, of the potential punishment available as a result of the bad acts. Punitive damages are included in addition to compensatory damages. In the previous example of an automobile accident, a judge or jury may choose to award punitive damages in addition to compensatory damages in a situation in which the defendant was solely at fault for the accident and left the scene prior to the arrival of law enforcement. In this case, the inclusion of punitive damages would serve as both punishment for the defendant who left the scene of the accident and to send a signal of deterrence to other citizens of the community.

In practical terms, the jury as a result of their verdict (or judge with the judicial finding) will convey to the parties their opinion of which party's case held more merit and the financial damages as a result of that decision. Additionally, in many civil cases, one or both parties may file a motion requesting an award of legal fees stating that they should not be required to pay for their own legal representation. The principle that each party needs to pay their own legal fees in civil court is well-established but, in an effort to make access to the civil justice system more equitable, laws have evolved that require one party to pay another party's legal fees in certain circumstances. The standard for the award of legal fees is high. The aggrieved party needs to prove to the court that the opposing party acted in bad faith—for example, filed a frivolous lawsuit—and the lawsuit should never have been filed.

The decision of the judge's finding or the jury's verdict is not final until the judge issues a final judgment and dismisses the case, either with prejudice or without prejudice. The law provides the judge's discretion, particularly in civil cases, to be used to potentially adjust any financial or other damages included within the jury's verdict. Once the judgment is entered into the court record, the lawsuit is final and the case is dismissed. If the case is dismissed with prejudice, the plaintiff is restricted from filing another lawsuit with the same court because the judge has ruled that the case is dismissed *on its merits*. If the case is dismissed without prejudice, this allows the plaintiff to correct any errors in the filing prior to re-submitting a complaint. If a case proceeds to trial, in the vast majority of instances any errors will be long corrected and a dismissal issued with the judge's ruling will be with prejudice.

> " *The principle that each party needs to pay their own legal fees in civil court is well-established but, in an effort to make access to the civil justice system more equitable, laws have evolved that require one party to pay another party's legal fees in certain circumstances.*"

After the judgment is issued, the losing party may file a motion for a new trial. The motion for a new trial may be filed in an effort to correct an error associated with the jury's verdict. For example, a jury may issue a verdict that favors the defendant but fails to award damages to the injured plaintiff—in which case, the plaintiff would have an incentive to file a motion for a new trial to seek to pursue damages with another jury. To be clear, this would require the hearing of the trial in its entirety—which is one reason judges are reluctant to rule in favor of motions for a new trial. In the timeframe between a jury verdict and judgment, the losing party can file a motion for judgment notwithstanding the verdict. This is essentially a request for the judge to issue a judgment that contradicts the jury's verdict. The standard for a favorable ruling in response to a motion for judgment notwithstanding the verdict is extremely high—

it must prove that no reasonable jury would issue the verdict based on the evidence and case law presented in trial. Often, if a party has decided to file a motion for judgment notwithstanding the verdict, the aggrieved party will simultaneously file a motion for a new trial—which is logical. If a jury issues a verdict not congruent with the facts, the reasonable accommodation is a new trial.

Aside from motioning for a new trial, losing parties, or even winning parties not receiving the judgment they desire, can appeal the decision of a civil trial. Depending on the case and jurisdiction of the civil trial, the losing party does not automatically have the right to appeal a decision, but rather, there must be a basis for this appeal.

The Appeals Process

The appeals process is available to both plaintiff and defendant in a civil lawsuit as a means of either correcting a reversible error or rectifying an abuse of discretion (by the judge in a bench trial). As such, the basis for an appeal is either a procedural error or an error in the judge's ruling. Appeals can be filed for either a concern related to a specific ruling—such as a judge's ruling regarding a discovery request or decision to either allow or restrict the introduction of evidence—or filed with the intent of correcting a final judgment. The intent of an appeal is to ensure justice is served in the case before the court as well as to solidify precedent by clarifying the law. The entirety of civil law, and criminal law for that matter, is based on precedence. As a result, the courts have a strong incentive to ensure a precedent that doesn't align with the court's interpretation of the law isn't able to be referenced in future lawsuits.

Given the fact that the law is based on interpretation, appellate law is considered a thorny and complex area of practice. In fact, if you have an issue to appeal, it's best to engage an appellate lawyer—someone who specializes in this area of the law—to handle the appeal. In larger law firms, the firm will have an appellate attorney on staff to assist with any efforts to appeal required by the firm's litigators. Otherwise, local attorneys in your area will likely have a relationship with an appellate lawyer who they can recommend.

> *Appeals can be filed for either a concern related to a specific ruling—such as a judge's ruling regarding a discovery request or decision to either allow or restrict the introduction of evidence—or filed with the intent of correcting a final judgment."*

An issue of law, not fact, must be the basis of an appeal and, additionally, the specific issue of law must be present in the court transcript. An issue of law that was not presented to the court cannot be used as the basis of an appeal. This bedrock principle of appellate law is logical and aligns with the concept of finality with regard to court rulings and judgments. If the law allowed for an issue that wasn't previously litigated, this would enable parties to continually bring new arguments to the court without restrictions. Given this concept, the court transcript is critical in any appeal. Savvy litigants, understanding this concept, will include references to any issue that may present a promising avenue of appeal in their filings and arguments to ensure the court transcript references the appealable issue.

> *An issue of law, not fact, must be the basis of an appeal and, additionally, the specific issue of law must be present in the court transcript. An issue of law that was not presented to the court cannot be used as the basis of an appeal."*

An appeal is essentially a petition asking a higher court to review an existing ruling or judgment from a lower court and issue a new ruling. Every litigant in civil court has a right to appeal (if there's a basis for the appeal), yet the vast majority of appeals never result in oral arguments. If a party decides to file a Notice of Appeal, this is followed by a brief—a written argument, and underlying documentation that supports the argument—detailing the decision they seek to be reversed. The other (non-filing) party subsequently has a prescribed time period to submit a response. The vast majority of appeals are decided by an examination of the written briefs—though sometimes the appellate court will request oral arguments from both sides. Appellate hearings don't include witness testimony, the introduction of new evidence, or any of the other standard mechanisms available in trial court. After all, appellate hearings are not retrials—the process of requesting a retrial is fundamentally different from the appellate process.

If the appellate court agrees with the lower court's decision, the issue is resolved (though the party that filed the appeal has the opportunity to file another appeal to an even higher court if available). If the appellate court rules in favor of the appeal and disagrees with the lower court's decision, a number of actions may occur depending on the particulars of the appeal. For example, the appellate court could order the lower court to conduct a new trial, correct the previous ruling or take any other appropriate action that can be considered judicial relief to the appeal petitioner such as include or exclude new evidence or revisit the case based on the higher court's ruling.

Appealing a judicial ruling or decision is significant in terms of both time and effort. Appeals are not cheap and require guidance due to the fact that they require the expertise of an appellate attorney who specializes in this area of the law. In other words, you'll need to engage and pay for a lawyer who will need to become familiar with all the particulars of your existing (or recently concluded) lawsuit and develop an appeal argument based on an issue of law. Additionally, similar to civil trial courts, the dockets of the appellate courts are typically overwhelmed. Odds are stacked against litigants seeking resolution through the appellate courts. It's difficult to obtain statistics regarding the percentage of appeals that are successful in the civil courts—but, anecdotally, an appeal is a significant challenge. The best practice is to conduct a similar business case analysis as recommended when filing a civil complaint. Assess the merits of the appeal, calculate the cost, estimate the potential payback, and make a decision.

Phase Six:
Post-Judgment
Activities

*"Sooner or later everyone sits down
to a banquet of consequences."*

— ROBERT LOUIS STEVENSON

Collections

At the end of the long road, it comes down to money. You've managed to navigate your way through the civil justice system and, at the end of your journey, there's a judgment that states the opposing party now owes you a financial sum. This could be the result of a favorable verdict followed by a judicial ruling or a settlement agreement—remember a settlement agreement is only enforceable once the court has accepted the agreement and dismissed the case with a judicial ruling. Either way, the next obvious question is, what now? Or, put more succinctly, how do you get your money?

Despite the amount of effort required to obtain an award of damages, the collection of the money (or any other concessions for that matter, but for simplicity's sake, we'll use the example of money) is not always easy though the process is fairly straightforward. If the opposing party—the party that owes money—is financially stable and healthy that party will usually pay the award in an effort to avoid any further costs such as additional legal fees or financial penalties associated with a failure to pay.

This may require a payment schedule, and patience on behalf of the winning party, but the court can be involved in securing arrangements to facilitate payment. On the other hand, if the opposing party—the party that owes money—does not have the capital to pay or simply refuses to pay, this is when this phase of the civil justice process can become stressful and frustrating for both parties—particularly the party awaiting payment.

Rules vary from state-to-state but, in most states, a winning party can conduct legal discovery activities—for example, requests for production and depositions—similar to discovery in a lawsuit. If evidence is found that the party failing to make payment has the financial ability to do so, the winning party can petition the court to garnish wages or other financial instruments such as bank accounts. Unfortunately, the process of collection itself can cost time and money as the winning party may be forced to hire an attorney or even a collection agency—who will likely require a percentage of the money ultimately collected—in order to enforce the judgment. The time period for collection varies by state. In some states the period may last as long as ten years but, again this varies by state, the time period can be extended for additional time if the winning party petitions for an extension with the court. The lengthy collection period is designed to ensure parties who are owed money as a result of a civil court judgment are paid—a party who may be unwilling or unable to pay initially may have a change of personal or financial circumstances years later that may create the conditions that enable that person to pay. Unfortunately, if at any time during the course of the collection period the party who owes money files for chapter seven bankruptcy protection, the party awaiting payment will be treated as simply another creditor by the bankruptcy court and may lose their ability to enforce the judgment. In other words, if the losing party files for bankruptcy the winning party may never get paid.

This brings us to one of the most important statements in this book: *If you think the opposing party will be unable or un-*

willing to pay if they lose in civil court, this factor needs to be included into the business case for the lawsuit. A judgment and award for damages is only as valuable as the opposing party's ability to make the payment or payments. If, in your estimation, the opposing party to your potential lawsuit does not have ability to pay if they lose, then it may not be worth the effort to file the effort regardless of how strong your case is or how egregious the opposing party's behavior was or is. Depending on the anticipated size of the award, this may require a best-guess assessment of the opposing party's financial circumstances. Does the other party have any assets that you know of—such as a house or an interest in a thriving business? Is the other party gainfully employed?

> *If you think the opposing party will be unable or unwilling to pay if they lose in civil court, this factor needs to be included into the business case for the lawsuit."*

Given this reality, it's oftentimes prudent to consider including other parties who may have more financial resources as a party in the complaint or counterclaim or identify well-funded organizations who may have an obligation to make good on any potential payment—such as an insurance company, for example, associated with a lawyer or doctor in a malpractice lawsuit.

Criminal Referral

A final note regarding post-trial activities: if, during the course of the trial, you've discovered potentially criminal activities by either the opposing party or a third party, you have the opportunity to provide law enforcement with this evidence as a criminal referral. It's important to remember that law enforcement is inundated with reports of crimes and often only has the resources to investigate the most egregious of situations. There's no guarantee that law enforcement will investigate your criminal complaint but it may be worthwhile to pursue.

Judicial Declaration of Action

In some very specific occasions, a judicial declaration of action presents an opportunity to secure clarity regarding a matter of the law as it's applied to the specific circumstances of controversy related to a potential lawsuit in a manner that saves both potential litigants and the court effort and expense. A declaration of action, also referred to as a declaration or declaratory relief, is a legal judgment that explains the rights and responsibilities of the parties involved in the controversy. Declaratory judgments are legally binding. By obtaining a declaratory judgment, a potential litigant will obtain clarity regarding their own rights and responsibilities as well as, potentially, the rights and responsibilities of other possible parties to a future lawsuit. With this clarity, a potential litigant will have a clear-eyed understanding on a potentially crucial aspect of the legal controversy which may inform the litigant's decision of whether or not to file an initial complaint.

Contract law is a great example of an area of the law where the pursuit of a declaratory judgment can inform a potential litigant's future actions. In this example, a disagreement may exist between two parties of a contract regarding a specific term within the contract or even whether or not the contract between the two parties is valid. In this situation, a plaintiff who thinks the terms of the contract have been breached by the other party can request a declaratory judgment from the court clarifying the terms of the contract as it relates to the rights and responsibilities of both parties as outlined in the specific contract. In this simple example, a future plaintiff—armed with the clarity afforded by the declaratory judgment that the contract between the two parties is valid—may use this legally binding judgment to inform their decision to file a complaint against the other party for breach of contract. Additionally, the plaintiff can reference the declaratory judgment to proactively invalidate the other party's defense that—in this example—the contract was not valid. In this way, the pursuit of a declaratory judgment allows the court to provide guidance to potential litigants regarding specific areas of the law which can be used to inform future action. In the example above, if the declaratory judgment determined that the contract between the two parties was not valid, the plaintiff would likely not proceed with the filing of their complaint which would save time and expense for both potential litigants as well as the court.

Appendix

Anxiety, Stress, and the Legal Process

*"Worrying does not take away tomorrow's troubles.
It takes away today's peace."*

— RANDY ARMSTRONG

Anxiety and increased stress levels are strongly correlated with major life events. The death of a loved one, a health crisis or serious illness, the loss of a job, or a divorce have been proven by the scientific community to precipitate a rise in an individual's anxiety levels. In fact, evidence suggests that even positive changes in a person's life—such as a voluntary job change, wedding, or the birth of a new child—correspond with increased anxiety levels. Significant events are, inherently, meaningful changes in life circumstances. By nature, most individuals desire order and stability—any change in the routine raises stress even if the person views the change as positive.

A slew of scientific studies have been published regarding the correlation between raised anxiety levels and major life events. There's a commonality of many of the other life events to the human condition: birth, death, weddings, divorces, new jobs, and new houses. We don't all experience each of these life events—and, certainly, we don't all experience each life event in the same way—but these life transitions are so ingrained in our society that most individuals can relate to many of them. The underlying message—major life events increase anxiety and stress—is easy to comprehend when given this context.

Legal entanglements aren't generally included in the list of life events associated with elevated levels of stress but, as anyone who's been involved in a lengthy legal battle will attest, they should be. Lawsuits are intrinsically open-ended as exhibited by the common legal strategy of utilizing the lack of a definitive conclusion as a component in negotiations. From a psychological perspective, the inability to predict the course or see an end to the event can induce elevated stress levels. The longer the stressful life period lasts, and the more difficult it is to identify an end date to it, the more likely the experience will result in physical, mental, or emotional symptoms associated with heightened stress and anxiety levels.

> *From a psychological perspective, the inability to predict the course or see an end to the event can induce elevated stress levels. The longer the stressful life period lasts, and the more difficult it is to identify an end date to it, the more likely the experience will result in physical, mental, or emotional symptoms associated with heightened stress and anxiety levels."*

Depending on the circumstances of the situation, a legal battle is often entangled with other stressful life events. An estate lawsuit may involve the death of a loved one. A family law dispute may be related to the dissolution of a marriage and child custody issues. Even a seemingly trivial legal impasse—such as a property line disagreement—may impact a person's sense of security in their home.

In addition, the uniqueness and potential stigma of being involved in a legal dispute—even if you are clearly the wronged party—may prevent discussion of the circumstances regarding a lawsuit with all but the closest confidantes. Most people can relate to marital troubles, work difficulties, and the challenges of raising children, but sharing the incremental wins and setbacks associated with a lawsuit isn't always the easiest topic to discuss in casual conversation. It's not easy to compare experiences or learn from others who've gone through the legal process. This social dynamic may lead to a sense of loneliness that can heighten already-elevated anxiety and stress levels.

On its own merits, a legal battle is unavoidably stressful. The lack of a concrete end-date, the uniqueness of each litigant's case, the inability to communicate with others in similar circumstances and the fact that many legal issues are strongly associated with already-stressful life events can result in an overwhelming psychological and emotional impact.

Individuals with existing elevated anxiety conditions, such as those with generalized anxiety disorder, may be more susceptible to experiencing elevated stress levels during the course of a lawsuit, but everyone is vulnerable to the physical and mental effects. This ingrained physiological response has, historically, served an important role in our efforts to survive and helped humans mobilize with biological reactions such as increased adrenaline to avoid threats. Yet, this important and previously healthy response can lead to unhealthy outcomes when the body is reacting, or overreacting, to dangers that aren't necessarily immediate. In these situations, the body's natural reactions transition from a healthy stressful response to an unhealthy level of distress.

Known as the "silent killer," elevated stress levels can result in a wide variety of cognitive, psychological and emotional repercussions. Often, changes in behavior can indicate raised stress levels and potential, harmful impacts. Behavioral indicators include the following:

- Decreased social contact with friends and family
- Decreased and impaired work relationships
- A sense of loneliness or abandonment

Physical manifestations of elevated stress levels are highly individualized and may include the following:

- High blood pressure or elevated heart rate
- Fatigue, decreased energy levels, a sense of agitation or restlessness
- Digestive issues, muscle tension or twitching, or teeth grinding

- Dizziness, lightheadedness, nervousness, or hyperventilating

The cognitive impact of prolonged, elevated stress levels may include the following:

- Intrusive thoughts, worrying, and a constant sense of foreboding
- Confusion, difficulty with concentration, and forgetfulness
- Negativity
- A sense of being overwhelmed, indecisiveness, and an inability to think clearly

The science behind stress research has demonstrated that a person's reaction to a stressful event, a series of stressful events, or a prolonged time period of uncertainty is unique to each individual. The same circumstances can elicit drastically different reactions from two different people. Some may experience symptoms of elevated stress immediately, while others may never feel the impact. In some individuals, the onset of symptoms of stress may be delayed.

Stress researchers have identified, and extensively studied, a number of methods for reducing stress levels and mitigating the known physiological, psychological, and emotional impacts of prolonged elevated stress levels. Similar to the onset of stress symptoms, stress reduction practices have also been found to be highly individualized. Each suggested practice that follows has been demonstrated to lower stress levels in studies but it's clear that each individual responds differently to each practice. Not all results are uniform—what works for some people may not work for others. Identifying the best stress reduction practices requires a degree of trial-and-error on the part of the practitioner. My suggestion informed by years of anxiety-inducing litigation is to ask you to exert the effort to determine the best way to mitigate the stress in your life—particularly during the course of a lawsuit that is, by definition, a time of heightened stress and vulnerability to the physical, emotional, and psychological impacts of stress.

> " *My suggestion informed by years of anxiety-inducing litigation is to ask you to exert the effort to determine the best way to mitigate the stress in your life—particularly during the course of a lawsuit that is, by definition, a time of heightened stress and vulnerability to the physical, emotional, and psychological impacts of stress."*

Known ways to cope with stress and reduce or mitigate the impacts include the following:

- *Exercise:* According to the American Psychological Association, exercise "forces the body's physiological systems to communicate much more closely than usual." Essentially, exercise is the body's chance to "practice" responding to a threat.
- *Meditation:* According to Dr. Elizabeth Hoge, a psychiatrist at Massachusetts General Hospital's Center for Anxiety and Traumatic Stress Disorders, "people with anxiety have a problem dealing with distracting thoughts that have too much power" and "can't distinguish between a problem-solving thought and a nagging worry that has no benefit." The link between meditation and the reduction of anxiety and stress is well established and supported by a wide variety of academic studies.
- *Yoga:* Studies have shown the combination of exercise, mediation, relaxation, and community present in many yoga practices "tame the stress response" according to the Harvard Medical School. The reduction of standing heart

rate, lowering of blood pressure, and increased respiratory function associated with yoga directly counteracts the physiological responses associated with increased stress levels.

- *Journaling:* Intrusive thoughts are a common symptom of stress. By committing those thoughts to paper, journaling can provide stress relief by ending—or, at least, pausing—the repetitive cycle of worry and provide an outlet to gain perspective.
- *Music playing:* The practice of making music lowers the stress response particularly when undertaken in a low pressure, recreational setting. Even simply listening to music has been found to result in similar brain responses and stress reduction benefits particularly in individuals with musical training.
- *Nutrition:* Certain foods can produce a calming effect while other foods can exacerbate stress symptoms. Foods with high caffeine content, high sugar content, or highly processed foods should be avoided. Individuals in stressful circumstances should increase consumption of foods with high omega-3 fatty acids (such as salmon, mackerel, anchovies, and sardines) and naturally decaffeinated teas with known calming properties such as chamomile. During times of extraordinary stress, take an inventory of your diet to determine potential foods to add or subtract to optimize your body's ability to react to stress and avoid periods of distress.
- *Therapy:* The negative impacts of elevated stress are a result of not only the stressful event or situation but also the manner of thinking about the circumstances. Psychotherapy and cognitive therapy help individuals "reframe" the situation and eliminate negative self-talk. These forms of treatment have been found to positively correlate with a reduction in the physiological impacts of raised stress levels.

In the context of a lawsuit, there are times when stress level peaks and wanes upon each participant depending on the state of the case and the position of each litigant at any given moment. The pressure to produce, and the associated stress, also shifts from one side to the other—in some instances multiple times through the course of the lawsuit. At certain points in the case, the plaintiff may shoulder the bulk of the stress while circumstances may change to shift the stress to the defendant. Being cognizant of the potential for physical, psychological, and emotional impacts, aware of the effects of the stressful legal situations upon oneself and purposefully acting to mitigate their impact can prove to be invaluable—in some situations, as valuable as a winning legal strategy.

> " *Being cognizant of the potential for physical, psychological, and emotional impacts, aware of the effects of the stressful legal situations upon oneself and purposefully acting to mitigate their impact can prove to be invaluable—in some situations, as valuable as a winning legal strategy.*"

A Personal Appeal: Legal Aid and Access to the Legal Courts for All

"Rather than justice for all, we are evolving into a system of justice for those who can afford it."

— JOSEPH E. STIGLITZ

The extent of income inequality and wealth concentration that defines the United States is currently at a level not seen since the Great Depression. This is a fairly well understood issue given the frequent studies published by prominent universities and advocacy groups. Not to mention the raft of articles that accompany the publication of each of those studies. A less discussed topic is the associated impact this has on the ability of individuals to access the legal system. Other trends such as declines in household savings, disposable income, and unstructured time exacerbate the situation. Developing a compelling legal case requires money and time. The basis of any legal strategy is to leverage any disadvantage the opposition may have, including their ability, or inability, to raise capital and fund a legal effort. If one side can outspend the other, it does so until the other side simply gives up.

A well-capitalized opponent can effectively deploy this strategy against almost any individual in our society. After all, only a small percentage of us have unlimited capital to dedicate to a lawsuit as demonstrated by myriad wealth concentration studies. The merits of the case become less important when you run out of money to build your argument. Yet, this strategy is most effective—and most troubling—when deployed against the most economically disadvantaged among us.

Lack of financial resources isn't the only barrier to justice. An individual needs to understand the extent of their rights and the avenues available to exercise those rights. If a person has a valid complaint but never pursues the issue, the lack of access to legal education and resources equals a lack of access to justice.

A critical difference between criminal and civil law is civil law litigants are not granted the right to legal counsel by the Constitution. (For additional information, Supreme Court decisions in *Lassiter v. Department of Social Services* and *Turner v. Rogers* are particularly relevant and enlightening). With a few well-defined exceptions in some jurisdictions, an individual is required to fund his or her own participation in the civil legal system. As a result, many individuals—particularly low-income individuals—are limited in their ability to access the civil legal system. The Legal Services Corporation—a nonprofit organization established by the United States Congress to monitor and address this issue—labels this phenomenon the "justice gap" and issues periodic reports documenting the issue.

> ❝❝ *If a person has a valid complaint but never pursues the issue, the lack of access to legal education and resources equals a lack of access to justice.*❞

To address the justice gap, a wide variety of national, state, and local legal aid and community clinics have been established. To be clear—some of these organizations are not limited in scope to civil law and also provide legal advice regarding criminal matters. According to a recent study by the Center for Law and Social Policy, civil legal assistance groups in the United States had $1.3B in funding available to address the justice gap at the beginning of 2013. Funding sources of such efforts include charitable donations from individual and foundations, state and local government, and public agencies (including a percentage of legal filing fees in some jurisdictions dedicated to funding legal assistance programs), legal community and bar association funding including so-called IOLTA funds (interest of lawyer trust accounts), and grants from the previously mentioned Legal Services Corporation. (Note: Grants from the LSC also include various restrictions for the use of the money and, as a result, some legal aid programs decide to seek funding elsewhere).

Legal aid organizations are dedicated to providing assistance to low-income individuals, but a universal income requirement standard has not been enacted to document standard income requirements for receiving client assistance from your local legal aid program. LSC-funded legal aid assistance programs, in general terms, restrict assistance to individuals at or below 125 percent of the Federal Poverty Guidelines. Most legal aid organizations that receive funding from non-LSC sources have significant discretion in their self-defined income eligibility requirements, though some funding sources include their own eligibility guidelines or requirements. LSC income eligibility guidelines are widely adopted as a general rule of thumb. Yet, it's important to remember that eligibility does not automatically equate to assistance. Not every person that qualifies on the basis of his or her income receives legal aid assistance. In a study published by the LSC titled "Documenting the Justice Gap in America: The Current Unmet Civil Legal Needs of Low-Income Americans," 50 percent of potential clients to LSC-funded organizations were turned away due to a lack of resources on the part of the assistance program. The study also estimated that there is one legal aid attorney for every 6,145 low-income individuals in the United States (the attorney-to-individual ratio within the general population is one attorney for every 429 individuals).

In short, demand for low-income legal aid assistance is far outpacing supply.

Legal aid assistance organizations provide legal advice on a wide variety of legal issues including labor and employment issues, housing and eviction concerns, accident and personal injury disputes, standard contractual issues, immigration cases, family law problems, and diverse contractual and discrimination issues. The delivery of this advice also varies and includes salaried legal aid offices, organized pro bono resources, legal advice and information hotlines, and law school clinics.

In more accessible terms, this translates to people helping people. Legal aid helps low-income individuals attempt to navigate some of life's most challenging and important issues during times when this advice is most needed. Legal aid assistance prevents people from being illegally evicted from their homes, unlawfully dismissed from their jobs, illegally deported from the country and separated from their families, and seeks to address the various manners of discrimination rampant in our society.

When you compare the justice gap among developed countries, it's apparent the United States' efforts to address this issue do not keep pace. A study published in the *Fordham International Law Journal* written by Justice Earl Johnson, Jr. titled "Equal Access to Justice: Comparing Access to Justice in the United States and Other Industrialized Democracies" documents this shortcoming of our society in great detail. It's true that this study was published in 2000 and, since that time, civil aid funding in the United States has grown significantly from $800M in total funding in 2000 to $1.34B in 2013. Yet, this growth in funding still pales in comparison to the capital and resources dedicated in other democracies to bridging the justice gap. The fact remains too many individuals are effectively being denied justice due to a financial inability to exercise their legal rights. The relative lack of funding in the United States to support the legal aid assistance groups ensures this travesty will continue. This translates to low-income individuals being evicted, deported, fired, discriminated against, and taken advantage of without the ability to invoke their legal rights, fight for themselves, and have their voices heard or their day in court.

By purchasing this book, you've already contributed to efforts to address this problem of inequality. The author donates a percentage of all profits from the sale of this book to our partners in the legal aid and justice reform communities (a list of our partners can be found on our website). Obviously, this is not enough. As mentioned earlier, 50 percent of all individuals that request help from Legal Aid assistance organizations in the United States are turned away due to lack of resources.

> " *The fact remains too many individuals are effectively being denied justice due to a financial inability to exercise their legal rights.* "

Anyone buying this book is most likely facing legal fees that are an unbudgeted expense. As such, this may not be the best time to ask you to support your local legal aid assistance program ... but it may also be the perfect time. Experience with the civil legal system only further demonstrates the evident need for additional funding for legal aid assistance programs. Please consider an additional donation to your local civil aid assistance program. By donating, you'll be bringing justice to your community, enabling the financially disadvantaged the opportunity to exercise their legal rights, giving voice to the powerless, and assisting the well-meaning folks within the legal community in fulfilling their mission of obtaining justice for all.

The truth and justice promised by our legal system become empty, hollow promises too often and to too many people when they find themselves in a position where legal remedies are required. Reality transcends lofty ideals. A donation to your local legal aid assistance program helps well-meaning legal professionals deliver a reality that coincides with the lofty ideals upon which our legal system was established.

If you're seeking ways to donate to this worthy cause, see the links below:

The Legal Aid Association of California (LAAC) is a statewide membership organization with more than 100 legal non-profit organizations that provide "critical legal assistance to low-income Californians and ensure equal access to justice." The mission of the LAAC includes advocating for additional funding for legal services in the state budget process, training legal aid providers, and creating a community of members to share resources, best practices and litigation strategies to help LAAC and their member organizations fulfill their joint mission. To donate to the LACC, please visit this link.[1]

Rhode Island Legal Services is dedicated to providing legal services and representation to low-income individuals and other eligible client groups. The non-profit organization's efforts to provide access to the justice system span a diverse set of challenges including family law matters, housing, employment, consumer issues, disability rights, healthcare, and elder law matters. To donate to the Rhode Island Legal Services, please visit this link.[2]

Legal Services Corporation is the country's largest funder of civil legal aid for low-income individuals. The 501(c)(3) corporation "distributes more than 90 percent of its funding to 134 independent non-profit legal aid organizations in every state, the District of Columbia and U.S. Territories." To donate to the LSC, please visit this link.[3]

A number of factors are used to determine an individual's ability to qualify for legal aid. Individuals who qualify for legal aid can include "indigent persons" as defined by the local courts, individuals with qualifying household incomes as compared to the federally recognized poverty level, victims of domestic abuse, immigrants, disabled veterans, persons living with HIV/AIDS, or community organizations that are working on behalf of disadvantaged or underserved communities. Eligibility for

---

[1] https://www.laaconline.org

[2] https://connect.clickandpledge.com/w/Form/b6169c43-a089-49fb-93ef-a06130db6c0e

[3] https://www.lsc.gov/donate-now

qualifying for legal aid assistance differs significantly based on state and county laws. An individual's case can also be subject to the resource constraints of the local legal aid providers. If you think you may qualify for legal aid assistance, please visit the Legal Services Corporation website[4] to find the provider in your geographic area.

---

[4] https://www.lsc.gov/about-lsc/what-legal-aid/get-legal-help

The Legal Literacy Project

The Legal Literacy Project is partnering with national and local civil aid service providers and justice reform advocacy groups to address the justice gap that exists in the United States. In a 2017 report[1], the Legal Services Corporation defined the justice gap as "the difference between the civil legal needs of low-income Americans and the resources available to meet those needs." According a report published by the Center for American Progress[2] in 2016, an examination of documents published by the Legal Services Corporation and the American Bar Association determined the following:

- "Congressional appropriations for the Legal Services Corporation were just $385 million in 2016."
- "In the early 1980s, by contrast, the corporation received more than $770 million annually."
- "Adjusted for inflation, the corporation's budget has decreased by 300 percent since 1981, even as the number of Americans eligible for aid has grown by 50 percent."

Without intervention, we can only expect this crisis situation to further deteriorate.

Access to the civil justice system for middle class Americans is also in a state of crisis. The Legal Services Corporation states that an individual or household's annual income can not exceed more than 125% of the federal poverty guidelines.[3] In 2015, an individual's annual income could not exceed $14,713 and a household's annual income could not exceed $30,313 in order

---

[1] https://lsc-live.app.box.com/s/6x4wbh5d2gqxwy0v0940s1x2k6a39q74

[2] https://www.americanprogress.org/article/making-justice-equal/

[3] https://www.lsc.gov/about-lsc/who-we-are

to be eligible for legal assistance from a LSC-funded legal aid service provider.

According to the Laffey Matrix, the average hourly fee in the United States for an attorney ranged from $333 / hour for an attorney with less than two years of experience to $655 / hour for an attorney with more than thirty-one years of experience. Given the complexity of the civil justice system, the cost of a typical lawsuit can easily become an unsustainable, financial burden for even the most privileged of middle-class households. In essence, the justice gap extends to the middle class—leaving access to the civil justice system as a luxury that only the wealthy can afford.

The goal of the Legal Literacy Project is to increase access to the civil justice system and support justice reform efforts. The Legal Literacy Project partners with legal aid service providers, justice reform advocacy groups and commercial legal service providers to address the justice gap via a combination of educational, advocacy and fund-raising efforts.

If your organization would like to contribute to this vital work, please contact the Legal Literacy Project.

The Justice Gap: Self-Represented Litigants and the Fight for Access to Justice

"Every day, countless Americans are in court grappling with life-altering challenges like foreclosure, eviction, debt and family instability—far too often, doing so without counsel." I not only have the right to stand up for myself, but I have the responsibility. I can't ask somebody else to stand up for me if I won't stand up for myself. And once you stand up for yourself, you'd be surprised that people say 'can I be of help.'"

— LORETTA LYNCH (FORMER UNITED STATES ATTORNEY GENERAL)

The expertise and experience of an attorney can prove invaluable in a person's effort to exercise their rights in a civil court. When a person is fighting for their home, their job, their children, their family, their healthcare or their safety, that person deserves the best representation possible. Some activists and experts argue that, given the stakes, representation in court is a human right. Unfortunately, thousands of hearings take place every day—thousands of cases every year—where one or more litigants are forced to represent themselves without the benefit of a lawyer. The primary reason for this is money—low income individuals and families simply can't afford to hire an attorney and finance a civil lawsuit. As a result, many individuals and families in this situation are forced to represent themselves in civil court. This often sets up a dynamic where one side is represented by an experienced and trained attorney and the other side is, essentially, figuring out the rules, procedures, tactics and strategies that comprise life in this country's civil courts on an ad-hoc basis. Self-represented litigants are much more likely than opposing party's represented by counsel to approach their case in a tactical and reactive manner, rather than the proactive and strategic approach employed by professional litigants. According to the New York Times[1], approximately 90% of landlords in landlord/tenant disputes are represented by an attorney while 90% of tenants nationally do not have a lawyer. Whether or not you have a lawyer as a tenant has a significant impact upon whether or not you win your case and, in landlord/tenant disputes, are able to remain in your home. For example, a different article from the New York Times[2] determined that self-represented tenants are evicted in 50% of cases while 90% of tenants who are represented by an attorney win their case and are able to stay in their homes.

> *Self-represented litigants are much more likely than opposing party's represented by counsel to approach their case in a tactical and reactive manner, rather than the proactive and strategic approach employed by professional litigants."*

The Legal Services Corporation (LSC)[3] was established in 1974 to ensure equal access to justice for the nation's low-income individuals and families. As of 2022, the organization distributed funding to 132 independent, non-profit legal aid programs that operate in 877 offices throughout the country. The LSC is a laudable organization with an admirable goal—ensuring access to justice for the nation's low-income—but, unfortunately, the demand for legal aid services far outweighs the supply of these services delivered by legal aid organizations. In 2022, the LSC published a report titled The Justice Gap 2022: The Unmet

---

[1] https://www.nytimes.com/2012/11/30/opinion/tipping-the-scales-in-housing-court.html?smid=pl-share

[2] https://www.nytimes.com/2016/09/23/opinion/a-right-to-a-lawyer-to-save-your-home.html?smid=pl-share

[3] https://www.lsc.gov

Civil Legal Needs of Low-Income Americans[1] that detailed the current state of this crisis of civil rights. The report provided the following details:

- In 2022, the LSC received less than half the funding the organization received in its initial year of operations (1974)
- According to the U.S. Census Bureau, more than 50 million American households qualify for legal aid assistance due to the fact that their household income is below 125% of the federal poverty threshold
- The LSC determined in their 2022 report that there is only one legal aid attorney for every 6,415 individuals eligible to receive assistance
- When considering the collective civil legal problems of low-income Americans, only 19% sought assistance for these problems in the past year (46% of low-income individuals who did not seek help referenced financial concerns as the reason for not seeking help)

The conclusion of this set of trends is that 92% of "substantial civil legal problems" in the lives of low-income Americans don't receive enough, or any, legal help. To make matters worse, the LSC estimates that only approximately 20% of all civil legal problems are reported. With this dynamic in mind, the situation is nothing short of a crisis.

The individual states have attempted to increase funding for legal aid organizations by committing the interest gained on lawyers' trust accounts to the cause. This is helpful from both fund-raising and awareness perspectives, but it simply isn't enough. Additionally, this approach relies on the prevailing in-

---

[1] https://www.lsc.gov/events/justice-gap-2022-report-release-unmet-civil-legal-needs-low-income-americans

terest rate associated with trust accounts and is subject to the vagaries of the overall economy.

> " The conclusion of this set of trends is that 92% of "substantial civil legal problems" in the lives of low-income Americans don't receive enough, or any, legal help. "

When we're discussing low-income Americans, we're really speaking about households with children, the elderly, veterans, people with disabilities, rural Americans and domestic violence victims. Each of these cases involve real people who experience tangible impacts to their quality of life as a result of the issues governed by the civil courts. In an article published by Richard Engler titled *Connecting Self-Representation to Civil Gideon: What Existing Data Reveal About When Counsel is Most Needed*[2], Mr. Engler found that self-represented litigants lose regularly in civil court even when the law is on their side. Additionally, the study chronicled the "stunning regularity with which unrepresented tenants lose in housing court." According to the 2022 LSC Justice Gap report cited previously, "1 in 2 (55%) low-income Americans who personally experienced a problem say these problems substantially impacted their lives—with the consequences affecting their finances, mental health, physical health and safety, and relationships."

The decrease in funding of the Legal Services Corporation and the associated reduction in funding for state and local legal aid organizations is not the only trend that is limiting low-income Americans' access to justice. Funding for state and local civil courts has also decreased. Additionally, the Constitutional right to a speedy trial in criminal cases ensures funding for

---

[2] https://ir.lawnet.fordham.edu/cgi/viewcontent.cgi?referer=&httpsredir=1&article=2321&context=ulj

criminal courts takes precedence over funding for civil courts. This further exacerbates the problem as reduced funding for civil courts can result in reduced hours of operations, reduced administrative staff and a decrease in court availability for civil litigants.

It's safe to assume that the longer this situation continues, the larger the justice gap in the United States will become. According to the LSC, the justice gap is widest for low-income Americans but, to a slightly less degree, this is a problem that also impacts middle-class Americans. Middle-income individuals and families are more likely, than their low-income counterparts, to seek legal help regarding issues that have a significant impact upon their lives, more likely to think they could find a lawyer if they need one and less likely to forgo legal help for legal problems. The justice gap is more profound in the lives of low-income Americans, but deeply ingrained within the lives of middle-class Americans. Previously, we mentioned that low-income Americans don't seek legal assistance for an appalling 92% of what they deem substantial legal problems in their lives—the 92% represents the justice gap in the lives of low-income Americans. For middle-class Americans, this justice gap figure is 78%. In other words, 78% of middle-class Americans fail to seek legal assistance regarding a substantial legal problem in their lives that could be resolved via the civil courts. Middle-income Americans are more likely than low-income Americans to seek legal help but in the vast majority of instances—78% of potential cases—these individuals and families decide to not pursue a remedy in civil courts that could be available to help resolve a substantial life issue.

What actions can we, as a society, take to address this situation, close the justice gap and ensure more low-income and middle-income individuals and families are able to access the civil justice system to resolve important issues in their lives?

Civil law reform activists advocate for a wide range of solutions that are often characterized as either supply-side or demand-side remedies. Supply-side solutions focus on increasing the supply of attorneys—or, at a minimum, access to legal information—for litigants while demand-side solutions focus on court reform to assist self-represented litigants in their efforts to navigate the civil justice system.

> " *The justice gap is more profound in the lives of low-income Americans, but deeply ingrained within the lives of middle-class Americans.*"

The essence of supply-side solutions is to increase access to legal assistance by increasing the number of lawyers available to assist low-income Americans or, alternatively, unbundling legal services to increase the number of low-income Americans who have access to at least some degree of legal expertise.

The National Coalition for a Civil Right to Counsel[1] advocates for and tracks the adoption of right to counsel efforts on a state-by-state basis, often referred to as "civil Gideon" (named after the Supreme Court case of *Gideon v Wainwright* that guaranteed anyone accused of a crime the right to a lawyer). The foundation supporting the civil right to counsel movement[2] is the concept that low-income individuals who are unable to retain an attorney should have access to a lawyer when the case involves a basic human right such as housing, health and safety, family law and child custody. To support these efforts, many states have created access to justice coalitions[3] that bring together multiple entities—such as the courts, the local legal-aid

---

[1] http://civilrighttocounsel.org

[2] https://www.americanbar.org/groups/bar_services/publications/bar_leader/2007_08/3206/gideon/

[3] https://www.americanbar.org/groups/litigation/committees/access-justice/commissions/

organizations and the local bar associations—to collaborate on efforts to increase access to justice for low-income Americans. States as diverse as Wisconsin, Massachusetts, Arkansas, North Carolina and Maryland have adopted the approach of right-to-counsel to be applied to cases that involve basic human needs.

Another supply-side solution is the unbundling of legal services. This approach advocates offering low-income Americans limited legal services—as a substitute for full legal representation—and is particularly targeted to self-represented litigants who require some level of guidance to navigate the civil justice system but can't afford to hire an attorney. Advocates say some level of legal guidance and advice is better than none and contend that unbundling is the most realistic approach to addressing the justice gap given the market dynamics—particularly the cost of legal services. Detractors say legal unbundling combined with efficient and effective self-help resources may work for individuals managing relatively simple and straightforward disputes but, in the event a case is complex and involves a complex area of the law, there is no substitute for full legal representation. Additionally, whenever a case involves a person fighting for their human rights, that person should have a lawyer advocating for them as is advanced by civil Gideon advocates.

> " *The foundation supporting the civil right to counsel movement is the concept that low-income individuals who are unable to retain an attorney should have access to a lawyer when the case involves a basic human right such as housing, health and safety, family law and child custody.* "

Demand-side reform advocates focus on specific changes and improvements to the operations of the civil court system in order to decrease the barriers to participation and increase access to justice. For example, Richard Larza—the founder of the

Self-Represented Litigation Network[1]—supports the idea of simplifying the litigation process particularly related to procedural and evidentiary rules that often confuse self-represented litigants unfamiliar with many of the details that govern civil litigation. A guiding principle of demand-side reform is to simply make it easier for a layperson to understand the process. This can take many forms including increasing the availability and quality of self-help resources, offering legal forms and instructions written at a level that maximizes ease-of-use and requiring judges serve as guiding resources for self-represented litigants with regards to process questions. Demand-side reformists also advocate focusing on areas of the law that feature a higher proportion of litigants not represented by attorneys—also known as "lawyer absent" areas of the law—such as divorce, child custody, bankruptcy and consumer debt and landlord/tenant law.

Supply-side and demand-side legal reform advocates agree that—in order to implement reform recommendations—the country needs to improve the collection of data and the quality of data reported by the more than 15,000 civil courts operating in the United States. The National Center for State Courts[2] administers and manages the Court Statistics Project[3]—which is the nation's best resource for annual state court caseload data. This data is used by various groups including the National Center for State Courts to fulfill its mission of increasing access to justice, advocating for racial justice, human rights and social justice and increasing the use of technology solutions to augment these principles. This is vital work which provides context regarding the operations of state courts and insight regarding potential reforms to increase access to justice. Reform is best

---

[1] https://www.srln.org

[2] https://www.ncsc.org

[3] https://www.courtstatistics.org

achieved when the current state of operations is well-understood—as a result, additional funding and resources need to be dedicated to these types of efforts in order to optimize civil justice reform efforts.

Yet, civil justice reform does not simply need an increase in funding, awareness or resources. More profoundly, civil justice reform requires an evolution in the manner in which the various stakeholders within the civil justice community—and the general public—perceive and imagine the vision and goals of the civil justice system. In order for the various reforms proposed to be widely adopted and newly conceptualized reforms to be proposed—in order for the civil courts to change in a way that truly increases the public's access to the justice system—our society needs to recognize the reality that millions of people each day have little choice but to engage within the civil justice system to resolve some of the most important issues impacting their lives. When viewed with this undeniable context it becomes clear that civil litigation is a human right that every person in the United States should be able to affordably and efficiently access. Until such time that our society views civil litigation as a civil right—and dedicates the money and resources required to fulfill this goal—the justice gap for low-income and middle-income Americans will remain.

Legal Specialties

"The successful warrior is the average man with laser-like focus."

— BRUCE LEE

The civil law is complex and resolving disputes via the civil courts requires the assistance of an attorney who specializes in the area of law most relevant to the matter. See below for a brief overview of legal practice areas that may be useful as a guide to identify the lawyer with the experience most applicable to your case. As a self-represented litigant, you're still allowed to hire an expert in the area of law to serve as an expert witness during trial—as such, the information below may be valuable in your attempts to leverage an expert's insight to explain particularly complex components of your case.

One nuance to keep in mind is the fact that many civil cases may span multiple practice areas. For example, a dispute regarding a contested inheritance may require the expertise of a trust and estate lawyer as well as a real estate specialist. As a result, many attorneys will have one practice area augmented by expertise in ancillary areas of the law based on their previous caseload.

- Adoption Law
- Alternative Dispute Resolution
- Bankruptcy
- Business/Corporate Law (Commercial Litigation)
- Class Action Litigation (Mass Tort Litigation)
- Civil Rights Law
- Consumer Law
- Elder Law
- Employment Law
- Entertainment Law

- Environmental and Natural Resources Law
- Family Law
- Financial Services Regulation Law
- Housing Law
- Immigration Law
- Intellectual Property Law
- Labor Law
- Malpractice Law
- Occupational Health and Safety Law
- Personal Injury Law
- Probate Law
- Real Estate Law
- Tax Law
- Tort Law
- Trust and Estate Law

The ability to litigate a case, regardless of the legal specialty, also requires unique skills, expertise, and approach. Each practice area described above includes attorneys who present cases in front of a judge and/or jury and other lawyers who practice law outside the confines of a courtroom. For example, you may require a lawyer who specializes in trust and estate law to write your will and trust documentation and this same person may also be qualified to settle the estate after the death of a loved one. Yet, if the estate is disputed and leads to a contested estate—and, ultimately, a lawsuit—you'd be best served to seek an attorney who has significant litigation experience in the area of trust and estate law. Both types of attorneys—estate specialists and estate litigators—provide a valuable skill for the appropriate circumstances. It's important to evaluate your legal situation and, if you expect a lawsuit to be filed or anticipate filing your own complaint, to find counsel with the *litigation* experience aligned with the practice area of the law that is most applicable to your legal dilemma.

Legal Resources

"The law is also a memory; the law also records a conversation, a nation arguing with its conscience."

— BARACK OBAMA, *DREAMS FROM MY FATHER: A STORY OF RACE AND INHERITANCE*

To assist with your continued pursuit to learn the law, understand your lawyer, and prevail in court, I've compiled a variety of resources below that span from the educational to the entertaining and the foundational to the groundbreaking. In addition to the resources listed below, you can also find information that is relevant to the specific area of the law in which your case falls via the websites of state bar associations and, even, the websites of law firms.

National Legal Associations and Information Repositories:

- American Association for Justice
- American Academy of Matrimonial Lawyers
- American Bar Association
- American College of Real Estate Lawyers
- American College of Trust and Estate Counsel
- American Immigration Lawyers Association
- Association of Attorney-Mediators
- Bloomberg Law
- Electronic Frontier Foundation
- Equal Rights Advocates
- Financial Crime Resource Center
- GoogleScholar
- Justia
- LexisNexis
- Maritime Law Association of the United States
- MuckRock

- NAACP Legal Defense and Educational Fund
- National Academy of Elder Law Attorneys
- National Association of Consumer Advocates
- National Association of Consumer Bankruptcy Attorneys
- National Association of Counsel for Children
- National Association of Criminal Defense Lawyers
- National Association of Estate Planners and Councils
- National Crime Victim Bar Association
- National Employment Lawyers Association
- National Elder Law Foundation
- National Lawyers Guild
- National Organization for the Reform of Marijuana Laws (NORML)
- National Police Accountability Project
- National Whistleblower Center
- Public Citizen
- Sunlight Foundation
- TheFOIAProject
- WestLaw

Above is a non-comprehensive list of advocacy groups that leverage the civil and criminal justice systems to promote social justice and civil rights. Groups have emerged to act on behalf of a wide variety of communities and with a focus on varied civil and criminal justice issues. See this website for additional details[1] and, if an organization's mission speaks to you, get involved!

---

[1] https://www.startguide.org/orgs/orgs06.html

Legal Websites and Blogs for Up-to-Date Arguments about the Law within the Legal Community[2]:

- ABAJournal
- Above the Law
- Arbitration Nation
- beSpacific
- EmployerHandbook
- FOIA Advisor
- FourthAmendment.com
- Glass Ceiling Discrimination Blog
- Jurist
- Lawfare
- Law21
- Open Law Lab
- Race and the Law Prof Blog
- Screw You Guys, I'm Going Home
- TheTMCA

Legal Fiction Books to Entertain, Educate, and Enlighten:

- *The Scarlet Letter* (Nathaniel Hawthorne): 1850
- *Bartleby the Scrivener* (Herman Melville): 1853
- *Bleak House* (Charles Dickens): 1853
- *A Tale of Two Cities* (Charles Dickens): 1859
- *Les Misérables* (Victor Hugo): 1862
- *Crime and Punishment* (Fyodor Dostoyevsky): 1866
- *Billy Budd, Sailor* (Herman Melville): 1924
- *The Trial* (Franz Kafka): 1925
- *An American Tragedy* (Theodore Dreiser): 1925
- *Their Eyes Were Watching God* (Zora Neale Hurston): 1937
- *The Ox-Bow Incident* (Walter Van Tilburg Clark): 1940

---

[2] https://www.abajournal.com/magazine/article/best_law_blogs_web_100

- *Native Son* (Richard Wright): 1940
- *Darkness at Noon* (Arthur Koestler): 1940
- *The Just and the Unjust* (James Cozzens): 1942
- *The Stranger* (Albert Camus): 1942
- *The Caine Mutiny* (Herman Wouk): 1951
- *By Love Possessed* (James Gould Cozzens): 1957
- *Anatomy of a Murder* (Robert Traver): 1958
- *To Kill a Mockingbird* (Harper Lee): 1960
- *Z* (Vassilis Vassilikos): 1967
- *The Paper Chase* (John Jay Osborn Jr.): 1971
- *The Book of Daniel* (E.L. Doctorow): 1971
- *Presumed Innocent* (Scott Turow): 1986
- *The Bonfire of the Vanities* (Tom Wolfe): 1987
- *A Time to Kill* (John Grisham): 1989
- *The Burden of Proof* (Scott Turow): 1990
- *The Firm* (John Grisham): 1991
- *Compelling Evidence* (Steve Martini): 1992
- *Primal Fear* (William Diehl): 1993
- *The Client* (John Grisham): 1993
- *A Civil Action* (Jonathan Harr): 1995
- *The Rainmaker* (John Grisham): 1995
- *The Testament* (John Grisham): 1999
- *Old Filth* (Jane Gardam): 2004
- *An Innocent Client* (Scott Pratt): 2013
- *Defending Jacob* (William Landay): 2013
- *The Children Act* (Ian McEwan): 2015
- *The Chamber* (John Grisham): 2017

Non-Fiction Books about the Cases that Changed the Law, Guides to Effective Advocacy, and the Moral Conundrums Inherent in the Law:

- *Gideon's Trumpet: How One Man, A Poor Prisoner, Took His Case to the Supreme Court—and Changed the Law of the United States* (Anthony Lewis): 1964

- *In Cold Blood* (Truman Capote): 1966
- *The Buffalo Creek Disaster: How the Survivors of One of the Worst Disasters in Coal-Mining History Brought Suit Against the Coal Company—and Won* (Gerald Stern): 1976
- *Local People: The Struggle for Civil Rights in Mississippi* (John Dittmer): 1994
- *We Wish the Inform You that Tomorrow We Will Be Killed With Our Families* (Philip Gourevitch): 1998
- *The Great Arizona Orphan Abduction* (Linda Gordon): 1999
- *The Moral Compass of the American Lawyer: Truth, Justice, Power and Greed* (Richard Zitrin and Caroline Langford): 1999
- *The Official Guide to Legal Specialties: An Insider's Guide to Every Major Practice Area* (Lisa Abrams): 2000
- *Arc of Justice: A Saga of Race, Civil Rights and Murder in the Jazz Age* (Kevin Boyle): 2004
- *The Rescue Artist: The True Story of Art, Thieves and the Hunt for a Missing Masterpiece* (Edward Dolnick): 2006
- *Storming the Court: How a Band of Law Students Fought the President—And Won (Brandt Goldstein)*: 2006
- *Justice: What's the Right Thing to Do?* (Michael J Sandel): 2010
- *The Rule of Law* (Tom Bingham): 2011
- *Storytelling for Lawyers* (Philip Meyer): 2014
- *End of Lawyers? Rethinking the Nature of Legal Services* (Richard Susskind): 2014
- Just Mercy: A Story of Justice and Redemption (Bryan Stephenson): 2014

Podcasts about Famous (and Not-So-Famous) Legal Battles, the Lawyer's Life, and the Ever-Evolving Legal System (Both Civil and Criminal):

- *Amicus* (Dahlia Lithwick)
- *Bloomberg Law* (June Grasso)

- *Criminal* (Phoebe Judge)
- *Evolve the Law* (Ian Connett)
- *In the Dark* (Madeleine Baran)
- *Lawyerist Podcast* (Sam Glover and Aaron Street)
- *Law360's Pro Say* (Amber Mckinney, Bill Donahue, and Alex Lawson)
- *Lawyer 2 Lawyer* (Robert Ambrogi and J. Craig Williams)
- *Legal Wars* (Hill Harper)
- *Reveal* (Al Letson)
- *Swindled* (A Concerned Citizen)
- *The Lawfare Podcast* (Benjamin Wittes and Susan Hennessey)

Ted Talks about the Law and the Legal System (Both Civil and Criminal):

- *Ai-Jen Poo: The Work That Makes All Other Work Possible*
- Alan Siegel: Let's Simplify Legal Jargon
- Bryan Stevenson: We Need to Talk About an Injustice
- Kimberley Motley: How I Defend the Rule Of Law
- Martha Minow: How Forgiveness Can Create a More Just Legal System
- Philip K. Howard: Four Ways to Fix a Broken Legal System
- Robert Palmer: The Panama Papers Exposed a Huge Global Problem. What's Next?
- Sandra Fisher-Martins: The Right to Understand
- Victoria Pratt : How Judges Can Show Respect
- Vivek Maru: How to Put the Power of Law in People's Hands
- William Black: How to Rob a Bank (from the Inside, That Is)

Movies about the Law, Lawyers, and Law Firms:

- *Adam's Rib* (1949)
- *12 Angry Men* (1957)
- *Witness for the Prosecution* (1957)
- *Anatomy of a Murder* (1959)
- *Judgment at Nuremberg* (1961)
- *To Kill a Mockingbird* (1962)
- *The Paper Chase* (1973)
- *Kramer vs. Kramer* (1979)
- *And Justice for All* (1979)
- *The Verdict* (1982)
- *Philadelphia* (1983)
- *The Accused* (1988)
- *Presumed Innocent* (1990)
- *Reversal of Fortune* (1990)
- *Class Action* (1991)
- *My Cousin Vinny* (1992)
- *A Few Good Men* (1992)
- *In the Name of the Father* (1993)
- *The Firm* (1993)
- *The Client* (1994)
- *Ghosts of Mississippi* (1996)
- *A Time to Kill* (1996)
- *Primal Fear* (1996)
- *The Rainmaker* (1997)
- *A Civil Action* (1998)
- *Erin Brockovich* (2000)
- *Intolerable Cruelty* (2003)
- *North Country* (2005)
- *Michael Clayton* (2007)
- *The Lincoln Lawyer* (2011)
- *Loving* (2016)
- *Marshall* (2017)
- *The Post* (2017)

Television Shows about the Law, Lawyers, and Law Firms:

- *Ally McBeal*
- *Better Call Saul*
- *Boston Legal*
- *Civil Wars*
- *Damages*
- *Franklin & Bash*
- *Goliath*
- *How to Get Away with Murder*
- *JAG*
- *Judging Amy*
- *L.A. Law*
- *Law & Order*
- *Law & Order: Criminal Intent*
- *Law & Order: Special Victims Unit*
- *Matlock*
- *Night Court*
- *Paper Chase*
- *Perry Mason*
- *Reasonable Doubts*
- *Scandal*
- *Suits*
- *The Good Wife*
- *The Good Fight*
- *The Practice*

Glossary of Legal Terms

Action: The series of facts that provides the legal justification for one person or entity to seek judicial relief from another person or entity (often referred to as the cause of action)

Admissible: The legal doctrine that determines whether or not evidence was both legally obtained and relevant to a legal case

Affidavit: A sworn and written declaration of facts used to present evidence to a court

Alternative dispute resolution (ADR): A method of resolving a legal conflict without litigation—often used to produce a faster and more cost-effective resolution compared to court system based litigation. Examples include arbitration and mediation.

Appeal: The legal process of requesting a higher court to reverse the judgment of a lower court based on a legal argument. New evidence is not allowed to be introduced during an appeal.

Arbitration: An alternative dispute resolution method in which both parties agree to grant authority to a single arbiter or board of arbiters to make a decision regarding a legal dispute outside the bounds of the traditional civil court. The process is similar to traditional litigation with the provision that the parties can agree to the rules of the process. Arbitration can either be binding—and enforceable as a court order—or non-binding.

Bench trial: A trial in which the judge is the sole decision-maker with regard to both question or law and question of fact. A bench trial is in contrast to a jury trial in which the jury is the decision-maker with regard to questions of fact and the judge decides the questions of law.

Burden of proof: The standard by which a party in a court of law seeking to prove a fact must meet in order for the fact to be legally established. For example, in civil cases the plaintiff has the burden of proof by a "preponderance of the evidence." Yet, during the course of a civil lawsuit the burden of proof can shift between plaintiff and defendant depending on the circumstances of the case and the moving party. "Preponderance of the evidence" is a specific standard in a legal court that holds that the moving party needs to prove there's more than a 50 percent chance that the assertion is true. Other standards of burden of proof exist—for example, "beyond a reasonable doubt" requires a higher standard (used in criminal cases) that demands there is no other reasonable explanation for the evidence presented to the court.

Cause of action: The combination of facts that provides a party to seek judicial relief within the civil courts. Also referred to as the legal theory that justifies the lawsuit.

Complaint: The legal action that provides the court with the facts and circumstances—the cause of action—that justifies a legal action. The complaint is the legal document filed by the plaintiff to initiate a lawsuit.

Count: In a complaint, the plaintiff provides the causes of action for the lawsuit. If a complaint has multiple causes of action, each unique cause of action is referred to as a count.

Counterclaim: A claim for judicial relief in a lawsuit filed against the opposition party in response to a prior claim. For example, a defendant in a civil case may file an answer to the plaintiff's initial complaint as well as file a counterclaim against the plaintiff.

Damages: A remedy, also known as a form of judicial relief, sought by a party in the course of a civil case. Damages are most often monetary awards and can be either compensatory or punitive. Compensatory damages seek to compensate the injured party and punitive damages are also often monetary and seek to both punish the offending party and deter the offending party, or the public at large, from repeating their offense.

Declaratory judgment: A judgment issued by a court that rules on the rights, responsibilities, and obligations of each and every party involved in the legal controversy before the court. Declaratory judgments are issued as a result of declaration actions, which are limited legal actions brought before the court designed to seek clarity regarding a legal matter of controversy either prior to or in conjunction with a legal complaint. Examples of issues where a declaration action may be appropriate are seeking the court's guidance regarding the terms of a contract, with regard to a potential contract breach, or the duties and required actions of a trustee.

Defendant: The party defending, or denying, the cause of action in a civil lawsuit

Deposition: Sworn testimony of a witness secured under oath recorded by a court reporter and outside of the confines of a courtroom. A critical component of the discovery process designed to introduce facts as evidence during a lawsuit

Discovery: The process in a lawsuit prior to a trial in which each party obtains evidence to support their legal assertions. Examples of discovery methods include depositions (sworn, spoken statements recorded by a court reporter), requests for production (documentation), interrogatories (sworn, written statements). and requests for admission of evidence.

Dismissal with prejudice: The dismissal of a lawsuit that prevents the same plaintiff from bringing a subsequent lawsuit to the court for the same cause of action

Dismissal without prejudice: The dismissal of a lawsuit that allows the same plaintiff from bringing a subsequent lawsuit to the court for the same cause of action

Docket: A listing of all the filings and proceedings related to a lawsuit

Duty of care: A legal obligation imposed, and accepted, by an individual or entity requiring that person to meet the standards required in their role. For example, a trustee for a trust has a duty of care to act in the best interests of the trust and the trust's beneficiaries.

Equitable: A request from a plaintiff for the court to take an action (also called an injunction) as relief, as opposed to a request for a monetary award

Hearsay: A statement made out of court and offered as evidence to support a party's case in the context of a lawsuit. The fact that the statement is made out of court, and not under oath, often makes the statement inadmissible as evidence to the court.

Injunction: A court order requiring a party to perform or cease performing an action. An injunction can also prevent an action from taking place prior to the initiation of the action.

Interrogatories: A component of the discovery process in which a party submits a list of questions to another party and that party is required to answer. The answers are considered submitted under oath and are admissible as evidence.

Joint tenancy: A shared ownership of a piece of property in which each owner has an undivided and equal interest in the property. Tenancy in common is a similar concept that allows for different ownership shares and different timeframes of ownership.

Judgment: A court decision (decree or an order)

Jurisdiction: The legal authority for a court to judge a case. In order to have jurisdiction, a court must have the ability to exercise control over the defendant, the property at issue must be within the court's control and the court must have the authority to decide the legal controversy at issue.

Jury Trial: A trial in which the jury is the arbiter with regard to questions of fact and the judge decides the questions of law. A bench trial is in contrast to a jury trial in which the judge is the sole arbiter with regard to both question or law and question of fact.

Litigation: The process of bringing an action to a court of law to resolve a dispute or enforce a legal right

Magistrate: A civil officer with the authority to administer and enforce the law. In some states, a magistrate is often responsible for resolving matters of the law in lower level courts.

Mediation: An alternative dispute resolution process that allows parties to discuss, and potentially resolve, their disputes with the assistance of a trained and neutral third party. Litigants may engage the services of a mediator to resolve the matter in a cost-efficient or timely manner, compared to a traditional court proceeding, or to ensure confidentiality.

Moving Party: The party who has filed the motion or petition with the court either verbally or in writing

Motion: A request to the court to obtain an order, ruling, or direction

Party: A person or legal entity that is named as a plaintiff or defendant on legal papers

Petition: A formal request made to the court in writing that requests a specific action of the court

Plaintiff: The party who files a complaint with the civil court to initiate the lawsuit

Pleadings: A formal written statement filed by a party with the court in the context of a lawsuit. Pleadings can either be complaints (specifying the cause of action) or answers (responding to the complaint).

Power of attorney: A document that authorizes one person or entity (the agent) the power and authority to act on behalf of another person (the principle) to make financial or medical decisions. A power of attorney can be broad or limited in scope with regard to the time period when the authority begins and/or ends and the scope and relevant circumstances in which the power is authorized.

Precedent: A court decision that is a guiding authority for deciding subsequent legal cases that involve similar facts. If the facts or legal issues in dispute in the subsequent case differ, the previous case cannot be precedent—which, inherently, results in further disputes regarding the similarity or dissimilarity of the facts and circumstances of the case cited as precedent.

Pro se: The Latin term ("in one's own behalf") describing parties representing themselves in court without representation from an attorney

Procedure: The rules by which the court conducts civil litigation including the pleadings, answers, discovery process, trial process, and appeal process

Res judicata: The Latin term ("a matter decided") to describe the principle that a cause of action has been decided in finality on its merits and not subject to litigation again by the same parties

Service of process: Delivery of legal documents to the person required to respond to the legal documents. Examples include a legal complaint or summons

Settlement: A legal and enforceable agreement reached by parties that results in the civil litigation from continuing to proceed as result of the agreement

Stare decisis: The Latin term ("to stand by things decided") to describe the legal doctrine that requires a court to adhere to legal precedent as demonstrated by legal decisions in court cases with similar facts and issues of law

Statute of limitations: The timeframe in which a civil action must be filed as prescribed by law. Different causes of action have differing statutes of limitations. The date when the statute of limitation clock begins to "toll"" is also extremely relevant when considering initiating a civil action. For example, a breach of contract complaint may have a four-year statute of limitations but the clock may only begin to toll (start) at the date when a party can be reasonably aware of the bad act(s) that caused the breach. The discovery of the bad act(s) may be well-beyond the statute of limitations when considering the date of the bad act(s)—but a party *may* still have standing to file a complaint based on the date of discovery of the bad act(s).

Subpoena: A written order to compel a party to provide testimony on a particular subject in a court-sanctioned venue to be used as evidence in a civil proceeding

Subpoena duces tecum: A type of subpoena that demands a witness produce relevant documentation to be admitted as evidence in a civil proceeding

Summary judgment: A judgment entered by a court in favor of one party over the other in response to a motion submitted asking the court for a ruling. A motion for summary judgment contends that, in review of all issues of fact and law presented to the court, the proceedings can cease as there is not a possible interpretation of the facts that would allow the dissenting party to prevail (win at trial). As such, summary judgment is a judgment without the need for a trial.

Tenancy-in-common: A shared ownership of a piece of property that allows each owner to own different shares (percentage interest) in a property for differing time periods. Joint tenancy is a similar concept that allows for each owner to have an undivided and equal interest in the property.

Tort: A act or omission (failure to act) that causes a harm or injury to another party (the act or omission can provide the basis for a lawsuit)

Transcript: A written record of court proceedings including a written record of verbal statements made in court sanctioned venue (for example, a transcript of testimony in trial or testimony during a deposition)

Trustee: A legal term to describe a person who acts "in a position of trust" with regard to property in which that person or entity has the responsibility to act in the best interests of the trust and the beneficiaries of the trust. The trustee has a duty of care with regard to the assets within the trust and the authority afforded to the trustee in the person's role as trustee.

Venue: The county (in state court) or district / division (in federal court) where a plaintiff files a lawsuit

Meet the Author

Matthew Madden is the author of Civil Law and the Civil Justice Process: A Client's Guide, Civil Law and the Civil Justice Process: A Guide to Self-Representation and the founder of the Legal Literacy Project. Matthew is currently writing the next book in the Legal Literacy Project series titled Financial Exploitation of the Elderly: A Family's Guide to the Nation's Most Shameful Crime. He's also writing a memoir about his family's experiences related to the financial exploitation of his father. Matthew and his wife Karri reside in Newport, Rhode Island.

The Legal Literacy Project: Other Books by Matthew Madden

Available Now:
Civil Law and the Civil Justice System: A Client's Guide
Learn the Law, Understand Your Lawyer, Prevail in Court

Coming Soon:
Financial Exploitation of the Elderly:
A Family's Guide to the Nation's Most Shameful Crime
Recognize the Clues, Respond to the Threat
& Protect Your Loved Ones

Connect with Matthew Madden

"When you learn, teach. When you get, give."

— MAYA ANGELOU

If this book was helpful in your efforts to navigate the civil justice system, please leave a review at the retailer where you purchased this book.

Also, I often write about legal issues from my unique perspective as a client. For additional content, please connect with me via the following platforms:

Website and Blog: https://legalliteracy.com/

Email: matt@legalliteracy.com